STUDYING LAW:
AN INTRODUCTION
TO LEGAL RESEARCH

SECOND EDITION

J. Clark Kelso

Professor of Law
University of the Pacific
McGeorge School of Law

1995

Matthew Bender
IRWIN

 Times Mirror
Books

MATTHEW BENDER & CO., INC.
EDITORIAL OFFICES
11 PENN PLAZA, NEW YORK, NY 10001-2006 (212) 967-7707
2101 WEBSTER ST., OAKLAND, CA 94612-3027 (510) 446-7100

LEGAL EDUCATION PUBLICATIONS

ADVISORY BOARD

To Kari, whose continuous love and support inspire my creativity.

PREFACE

This book is for use in an introductory course on legal research. The materials include this book and a set of computer exercises. This course has been designed so that you may proceed at your own pace, although many legal research professors will give you specific deadlines and assignments.

You will be learning in this course a certain amount of basic bibliographic information. That is, you will be learning about a few of the basic sources of law available to you in the library. You will also be learning in this course some of the basic skills needed to become a competent researcher. You will be learning about the process of legal research.

Bibliographic information can be imparted to you entirely by text. You will develop skills only by practicing them in the library itself. Unlike many other legal research books, I have deliberately omitted illustrations of what sample pages in law books look like. My experience — including my own behavior in law school — has been that the illustrations encourage students to read the legal research text at home and thereby make it easier for them to avoid setting foot in the library until actual library exercises must be done.

I have become convinced that a better way to teach bibliographic information is to encourage you to read this book while in the library actually comparing the text of this book to what you can see in a real law book. As you will see in Chapter 2, the book advises you to retrieve specific books from the library shelves while reading this book. Getting your hands on the actual law books may help you remember what books actually exist. Throughout this book, you should follow that pattern.

The computer exercises have been in use now for over five years. They include both multiple-choice questions to test your knowledge of material in the book and library research exercises that give you an opportunity to begin practicing and developing your research skills. You should take the first set of computer exercises after completing chapter 1.

I owe thanks to my colleague, Professor David Miller, for reviewing an early draft of the book, as well as to former McGeorge Legal Writing and Research Instructors Harriet Cummings, Elizabeth Miller, Sarah Pattison, and Terry Thurbon, for their constructive suggestions. Alan Diefenbach, a Reference Librarian at Harvard Law School, also contributed substantial insights and encouraged me to move forward with this work.

J. Clark Kelso
Sacramento, California
December, 1994

Table of Contents

Chapter 1
Introduction to Legal Research

Chapter 2.
Sources of the Common Law

Page

Chapter 3.
Computer-Assisted Legal Research

Chapter 4.
Legal Digests

Chapter 5.
Secondary Sources

CHAPTER 1

INTRODUCTION

A. The Lawyer As Researcher

Lawyers assume many different roles in serving the needs of society, as judges, arbitrators, mediators, advisors, legislators, and teachers, to name just a few. Certainly the greatest percentage of lawyers serve society by representing the interests of individual clients. According to a 1988 report, 72% of the half-million or so lawyers in the United States were engaged in private practice. Almost half of the private practitioners practiced alone or in small firms with no more than 10 attorneys.

Whatever role a lawyer assumes in society, competent performance in that role requires a solid foundation of information about the law on which to build. The process of systematically collecting information about the law is the process of legal research.

Learning how to research the law is one of the most important skills you will develop during your first year of law school. The ability to research the law on your own makes you independent of other lawyers. It gives you the ability to develop your own legal arguments and your own theories of the law.

Suppose, for example, a client enters your office with a complaint about a neighbor who has erected on his property a fence that blocks out the sun. Can the client do anything about it? Does the client have a cause of action against his neighbor? What remedies are likely to be available from a court of law? The only sure way to determine if a cause of action exists and, if one does, to determine what must be alleged in a complaint and proved to a court, is to research the issue under the law of the appropriate jurisdiction.

Suppose that you are trying to negotiate a computer software license for a bright young programmer. Unless you know exactly what rights the federal copyright law gives to computer program authors and how courts have interpreted those rights, you will not be able to represent your client's interest to the fullest. Legal research is the method by which you will gain that knowledge.

Finally, suppose that you are engaged in drafting significant legislation or administrative rules to secure public safety, protect the environment, implement health care reform, or to address any one of the host of important public policy issues of the day. Unless you understand the full range of existing statutory and administrative rules governing the subject matter, your efforts at reform will be short-lived. Legal research is the process you will use to discover the statutes and rules that already exist and the way in which courts have interpreted and applied those statutes and rules.

(Matthew Bender & Co., Inc.) (Pub. 776)

The materials presented in this book are introductory. Thus, you will not be exposed in this course to many research sources that a practicing lawyer might use. This course will, however, introduce you to the tools you will need to do basic legal research, including the most commonly used sources of legal materials. You will also learn in this course how to use a few of the major computer-assisted legal research systems which now are widely employed by practicing lawyers.

Just as important for the long career in law which lies ahead of you, the approach to legal research you begin developing here will carry over into other legal research situations and sources not covered in this book. You are thus learning more than bibliographic information. You are learning a systematic process and approach to gathering information about law, a process and approach that will serve you well throughout your career.

B. Law-Makers

Since our subject is legal research (in contrast, for example, to sociological or scientific research), our focus will be on those institutions in society that make law. Laws are made at many political levels and by many different institutions. We have, for example, international law, federal law, state law, county law, municipal law, and even neighborhood law. At each level, there are different juridical bodies that make the law and different challenges to researching the law.

In these materials, you will be introduced to law-making at the federal and state levels by courts, legislatures, and administrative agencies, and at the international level by sovereign nations, the United Nations, international tribunals, and other international organizations.

1. The Courts

The primary function of a court is to decide disputes between members of a society using procedures that are generally accepted as fair. In a phrase, a court's primary function is "dispute resolution."

The methods of dispute resolution are as varied as human imagination and intelligence. Until the middle of the 1800's, dueling was tolerated in many countries as an acceptable means of resolving private disputes. The precursor of duels in English history was trial by combat. Other historically permissible means of "truth-finding" and "dispute-resolution" included:

Divine intervention, in which the accused was usually placed in the position of killing herself (for example, by drowning in a lake) or saving herself (by coming out of the lake) only to be found therefore guilty and put to death for failing to trust in divine intervention to save her from drowning.

Compurgation, in which the accused could avoid punishment by giving an oath that she was not guilty and procuring the oaths of eleven neighbors that they believed the accused's oath.

Torture, in which a confession was extracted by physical force.

Modern society has rejected these violent methods of resolving disputes. Except in limited circumstances where a person may use force to defend oneself or others, peaceful means are now employed to resolve private disputes. Even among sovereign nations, principles of international law limit the circumstances in which war is legally permissible. *Compare* U.N. Charter Art. 51 (regarding self-defense) *with* Art. 33 (regarding pacific settlement of disputes). State sponsored torture and terrorism certainly exist, but are widely condemned as inhumane and illegal under principles of international law. *See, e.g., Filartiga v. Pena-Irala*, 630 F.2d 876 (2d Cir. 1980) (holding that state sponsored torture violates customary norms of international law).

Instead of resolving disputes by physical battles, societies around the world now provide for resolution of many public and private disputes by legal "battles," oftentimes in a court of law. Courtroom battles better attain the worthy goal of resolving a dispute on its merits rather than on the physical strength of the combatants. Although physical strength has become largely irrelevant to dispute resolution, the competence of the lawyer still has, in many cases, an important influence on the final outcome. Thus, the ideal of dispute-resolution solely on the basis of the merits is attained only to the extent that each disputant is able to secure an attorney of sufficient competence so that each disputant's interests are adequately and equally represented.

Counsel's ability successfully to research the law is one of the important equalizers. Both sides of a dispute have equal access to the books which contain the law. If counsel for both sides is competent in legal research, decisions are more likely to be based upon the merits of the dispute. By contrast, if only one counsel is a competent researcher, a court's decision may end up being the result more of incompetency of counsel than of an appraisal of the merits in light of all of the law.

There are many means of private dispute resolution other than court action. Most disputes are no doubt resolved simply between the parties or in a lawyer's office without the intervention of an independent judge. A good lawyer will do everything possible to avoid the expense and inconvenience of litigation. If negotiation is unsuccessful, the parties may turn to arbitration before considering court action. Arbitrations are something like trials before a court, but they are typically less formal, less time-consuming, and less expensive. Parties may also consider mediation, in which a neutral mediator attempts to forge a compromise position to which all parties agree. Other forms of appropriate dispute resolution (e.g., mini-trials or a combination of mediation and arbitration called "med/arb") are being developed all of the time.

For purposes of this course, we shall not be concerned with these more informal, private methods of dispute resolution. That is not because those methods are not as important as adjudication by trial. In fact, quite the contrary is true in practice; adjudication by trial is usually the option of last resort. We nevertheless will not focus on informal dispute resolution because, at present, informal adjudication only rarely leads to published materials that may be the subject of research. Indeed, part of the attraction and flexibility of many of these informal systems of dispute resolution is the absence of binding decisions in prior disputes. The publication of decisions that could be the subject of research would potentially undermine some of that flexibility. Furthermore, many parties enter mediation or arbitration precisely to avoid the publicity associated with a court trial.

(Matthew Bender & Co., Inc.) (Pub. 776)

Resolution of a dispute by a court, by contrast, is more likely to lead to publication of a written opinion explaining the court's decision. The body of written court opinions may then be the subject of legal research. We research prior opinions not only because "they are there," but also because in our "common law" system, decisions by prior courts create binding precedents or persuasive authority which future courts may respect and follow.

You are probably already aware that the phrase "common law" has many different meanings, depending upon the context. For example, "common law" may refer narrowly to decisions rendered by certain courts in England in the 18th century. In other contexts, "common law" refers to the law of the several states (as opposed to federal law). For purposes of legal research, the phrase "common law" means simply judge-made law found in the published decisions of courts. The common law so defined can be found in the thousands of case reporters in the library. In the next four chapters, you will learn how to find the common law relevant to a legal research assignment.

We define "common law" as "judge-made law" in order to distinguish it from statutes and administrative regulations, which are enacted by a legislature and administrative agency, respectively, and which are published in sets of books quite different from case reporters. As you will learn in later chapters, researching statutory or administrative issues is quite a different thing from researching the common law.

2. The Legislatures

Courts make law in the context of deciding specific disputes between litigants, and each case is dealt with as it arises. Legislatures, by contrast, usually act with an eye more to resolving an entire class or set of disputes that may arise in the future. It is true, of course, that legislatures sometimes act to resolve past disputes (e.g., recent federal legislation provided compensation to Japanese who were interred in camps during World War II). It is much more common, however, for a legislature to act prospectively and to act with respect to a large number of potential future disputes. For example, the Communications Act of 1934 created the Federal Communications Commission to resolve future disputes between radio and television stations over access to the public airwaves.

In our system of government, courts are required to give effect to legislation so long as it is constitutional. The legislature is supreme. Thus, you must always have in mind when doing research — even common law research — the possibility that a statute may exist which controls. Your research will not be complete until you determine that there is no statute (federal or state) which governs the issue you are researching.

Legislatures act by passing legislation. In general, an act passed by the legislature becomes law when signed by the chief executive or when enacted over the chief executive's veto. Laws then are assembled in codes, which are organized by subject matter for ease of use. The codes are heavily indexed so that a lawyer may readily determine whether any statutes exist on a particular subject matter.

Most legislation goes through a rigorous process of review before being voted on by the legislature. Consideration of an act by the full legislature usually comes after public hearings before legislative sub-committees and committees. These hearings are designed to educate the members of the legislature about what the problem is and about the best way to solve it. The reports drafted by these committees, as well as many other related documents, make up a "legislative history" for a particular enactment. This legislative history may contain hints (or even specific answers) as to what the legislature intended when it enacted a particular statute. You will learn in this course how to research the legislative history of a statute as an important step in understanding its meaning.

3. The Administrative Agencies

Congress is not the only institution at the federal level that enacts rules to govern future conduct. The Constitution describes only three branches of government, and only the Congress is explicitly authorized to enact law. But Congress, overwhelmed by the vastness of the federal government's modern responsibilities, has, by the enactment of thousands of statutes, created a "fourth branch" of government, administrative agencies, and has clothed those agencies with significant law-making power. The rules enacted by administrative agencies are assembled in their own codes, and there is a somewhat less voluminous legislative history for administrative rule-making.

Because Congress has authorized administrative agencies to enact rules, courts are required to follow administrative rules in much the same way that they are required to give effect to statutes. Specifically, courts must give effect to administrative rules unless (1) the rules are outside the administrative agency's statutory authorization, or (2) the rules are unconstitutional.

Many administrative agencies also act as courts in resolving private disputes concerning matters within the agency's area of expertise. The decisions rendered by the agency are then reported in special administrative law reporters. The decisions are usually reviewable by appellate courts.

Although administrative agencies act as both quasi-legislatures and quasi-adjudicators, research into administrative regulations and administrative decisions is generally more difficult than research into statutes or cases. The available sources are less fully developed and tend to be less convenient to use. The most useful research sources are often specialized publications that report about all of the activity of one administrative agency. For example, the Labor Law Reporter, a looseleaf publication produced by the Commerce Clearing House ("CCH"), reports rules enacted and decisions rendered by the National Labor Relations Board as well as labor law decisions of federal district and appellate courts. These looseleafs are the sources used by attorneys who regularly practice before a particular administrative agency.

Administrative agencies exist at the state and local level as well, and lawyers increasingly are finding themselves litigating important matters before state administrative law judges. Reports of state administrative rule-making and adjudication are even less well developed than at the federal level. As we enter the information age, however, we can expect a more thoroughly developed body of state administrative law. Fortunately, most states are following the basic pattern established by federal administrative agencies, which means that research skills developed for federal agencies will probably carry over into researching state administrative law.

4. International Law

Fifty or one hundred years ago, it would have been extremely rare for a private practitioner to have need to research issues involving international or transnational law.

Public international law, or the law of nations, was primarily limited to treaties between sovereign nations governing the obligations which sovereigns had to each other. The terms of treaties and principles of international law were of interest to government lawyers working in the White House or in the Department of State, but only infrequently were relevant to resolving private disputes.

Private international law, also known as "conflict of laws," is the set of principles and rules that, in the context of a private dispute which crosses international borders, answers the questions "in what court and by whose law should this dispute be resolved?" Fifty or one hundred years ago, principles of private international law would have been important to global corporations and to a few world travellers, but would have been irrelevant to the lives and legal problems of most Americans.

All of this has changed, and problems involving both public and private international law are now faced regularly by private practitioners around the country. This change is the result of three developments. First, the creation and growth of the United Nations and its many affiliated organizations has fostered the creation and growth of general principles of international law that govern not only the relation of sovereigns to each other, but also govern the relation of governments to people.

Second, faster and safer international transportation systems and the development of a global communication system has dramatically increased the daily interactions which people in one country have with people in other countries. People are thus more likely today to have problems that cross international borders.

Third, countries have increasingly entered into bilateral and multi-lateral agreements and treaties that regulate private transactions which cross international boundaries. For example, there now is a Convention for the International Sale of Goods that regulates purely private transactions in goods between persons from different countries which have signed the Convention.

Because of these developments, private practitioners today find themselves consulting sources of international law with much greater frequency. A competent legal researcher needs to know the basics of researching treaties and other works of international law.

C. Computer-Assisted Legal Research

Until the late 1970's, all legal research was done using books. Today, computers are used to perform in seconds research tasks that used to take hours or days or, in some cases, could not be done at all. The two leading computer research systems are LEXIS and WESTLAW. These systems are not yet capable of completely replacing book research, however, and book research remains competitively priced for many purposes (particularly because of the huge capital expenditures already invested by law offices in law books). That is why you must learn both book research skills and computer research skills. Whether computerized research will ever entirely replace book research remains an open and hotly debated question.

There has been a debate among legal research educators about whether computer research should be taught after book research or at the same time as book research. Initially, most legal research teachers believed that students should first learn the traditional methods of legal research before being exposed to computer research. More recently, several experienced and respected scholars of legal research have concluded after systematic study that students generally learn research skills better if both methodologies are taught at roughly the same time. In these materials, you will have the opportunity to learn both book research skills and computer research skills at the same time and should get a better appreciation of the comparative strengths and weaknesses of these two systems.

Beginning in the late 1980's, many law book publishers began to enter the computer age by putting significant sources of law on CD-ROMs which could then be searched in much the same way that searches are performed on LEXIS and WESTLAW. LEXIS and WESTLAW are thus not the only computerized legal research systems. This book discusses only LEXIS and WESTLAW because these two systems are, at present, the most widely used systems and because the basic principles of performing computerized legal research on these systems will carry over into performing research on other computerized systems.

D. Using The Library

The fact that you have been admitted to law school indicates that you possess certain minimum abilities and knowledge. One of the skills that we assume you have (and that we therefore do not formally teach) is an ability to use a library. Library skills include such things as how to use a card catalogue (in many libraries, a computerized card catalogue), how to locate a book given its call number, how to use an index or table of contents, and how to get the most from your librarians by interacting with them in a courteous manner. If you think you do not have these skills, you should probably ask a librarian (courteously!) for a tour of the library and an explanation of how to use the library's resources before you continue in this book. A tour and explanation will probably take less than an hour, and it will enhance your understanding of these materials as well as save you much stress when you start doing research exercises in the library.

In addition, you may discover when you begin to do the library research exercises that you need some help. When you need help, the Reference Librarian is the first person to whom you should turn. Don't be afraid or embarrassed to ask your Reference Librarian for assistance. Many of your professors routinely ask for such assistance, and there is no reason for you to neglect this important research resource. Your Reference Librarian can save you literally hours of frustrating and wasted time.

CHAPTER 2

SOURCES OF THE COMMON LAW

A. Introduction

In the next several chapters, we shall be concerned with researching the "common law." As explained in Chapter 1, when the words "common law" appear in this book, they refer most directly to judge-made law which appears in the reported decisions of the courts. When researching the common law, the most important question is, "What have courts in the past done?" The answer to that question, more often than not, will be the best indicator of what a court would do tomorrow.

Put yourself in the shoes of a fledgling attorney whose assignment is to research the common law concerning a particular legal issue or fact situation. You've been instructed by the senior associate to do exhaustive research, encompassing decisions from all American jurisdictions and all times. You've also been told that your research will be used in an ongoing litigation in a particular court, which the senior associate has identified for you (e.g., the Superior Court of the County of Orange in the State of California), and that your research should thus be concentrated initially on those decisions that will be most influential in the particular court identified.

In your new role of fledgling-attorney-with-research-assignment, you face at the very beginning two questions: First, how do you know which court's decisions are most likely to be followed in the particular court that the senior associate identified? Second, how do you find the decisions from that court, or any other court, that are relevant to the legal issue or fact situation you have been instructed to research? In Chapters 4 and 5, we shall address the second question. In this chapter, we shall be concerned only with the first question.

Let's assume that you have before you a pile of decisions from different jurisdictions and different courts all dealing with the same issue you have been instructed to research. You pick up the first case in the pile. Restating slightly our first question above, how do you know whether that decision will be respected and followed by the court identified by the senior associate, that is, the court that will hear and decide your case?

The starting point for answering this question is to consider an additional question: Is the decision that you have found a precedent in the identified court or merely persuasive authority? Precedents are those prior court decisions that a court has a general obligation to follow. Persuasive authority includes virtually all other writings, including opinions from others courts and scholarly writings, that may be used to persuade a court to adopt a particular rule of law. Given these descriptions, it should be clear that precedents are much more influential and have much greater predictive value than persuasive authority. When you are researching the law for

(Matthew Bender & Co., Inc.) (Pub. 776)

use in a particular litigation in a particular court, you hope to find cases that will be considered precedents by that court.

Whether a prior opinion constitutes a precedent in a particular court is determined solely by the relationship between that court and the court which issued the prior opinion. Precedents within a particular court are those prior decisions rendered either by the same court or a higher court within the jurisdiction.

For example, if you find yourself handling an appeal in the United States Court of Appeals for the Second Circuit, prior decisions by that court and the Supreme Court of the United States would be considered precedents. Prior decisions by the Supreme Court would be considered binding precedents or mandatory authority, which the Second Circuit would have an obligation to follow. Prior decisions by the Second Circuit would be entitled to a great deal of respect pursuant to the doctrine of stare decisis. Stare decisis, the principle that precedents should ordinarily be followed, helps bring stability and fairness to our common law system.

Decisions from lower federal courts or court from other jurisdictions would not be precedents in the Second Circuit. Thus, for example, decisions by the United States District Court for the Southern District of New York (a trial court from which appeals are taken to the Second Circuit) are not precedents in the Second Circuit; they are only persuasive authority. Decisions from other federal appellate courts, such as the Ninth Circuit Court of Appeals, would also not be precedents in the Second Circuit, but would be only persuasive authority.

As another example, suppose you are litigating in a state trial court in the County of Los Angeles, California. Precedents in this court would include all decisions rendered by the California Court of Appeals and the Supreme Court of California, and, with respect only to federal issues, decisions by the Supreme Court of the United States. Decisions from courts in other states would not be precedents in the California trial court; they would only be persuasive authority. Even decisions from a federal district court sitting in the County of Los Angeles would not be precedents, since the federal district court is considered to be an entirely separate jurisdiction from state courts.

These definitions and examples of precedent and persuasive authority may be somewhat different from what you have been taught in other classes. For example, you may have heard that any decision rendered on the same or similar facts may be a "precedent" and that there are (1) "binding precedents" (which are decisions on the same or similar facts rendered by the same or a higher court within the jurisdiction) and (2) "persuasive precedents" (which are decisions on the same or similar facts rendered by lower courts or courts in other jurisdictions). Although this terminology is adequate for some purposes, a California court would be somewhat shocked if you argued to it that a decision from a New York court or an English court was a precedent in California. It is a New York precedent or an English precedent, but it is most certainly not a California precedent. The New York decision is only persuasive authority in California.

As the above makes clear, a court's jurisdiction is the single most important factor in determining whether a relevant decision will be followed by a later court. A relevant decision from a state's highest court is very likely to be followed by a lower court within that state. Indeed, the lower court is ordinarily obliged to follow the decisions from the highest court within the jurisdiction and has no discretion not to follow those decisions. By contrast, a relevant decision from the highest court of another state is not nearly so likely to be followed.

There are, of course, other factors that affect the precedential weight of a decision ("weight" being just a shorthand way of indicating whether the decision is likely to be followed). These other factors include (1) the reputation of the judge who rendered the decision, (2) the age of the decision, (3) the completeness of the analysis supporting the decision, and (4) the existence of a convincing dissent. These factors, and this list is far from exhaustive, are obviously more intangible than the mechanical process of identifying the right court, but they are real factors nevertheless. They are factors a good practitioner must become familiar with in the jurisdictions and courts in which he or she practices. In these materials, however, we shall limit our consideration to the first and usually most important factor — the jurisdiction of the court.

You will learn in your course on Civil Procedure that the word "jurisdiction" has many different meanings depending upon the context in which it is used. Here, we are using the word "jurisdiction" to refer to the place a particular court has within the hierarchy of courts. In general, you can visualize the hierarchy of courts on a horizontal and vertical axis. As for the vertical axis, some courts are higher than other courts (e.g., the United States Supreme Court is higher than the United States District Courts). There is also a horizontal axis, however, where courts are of equal stature. For example, the First Circuit Court of Appeals is a federal appellate court on the same horizontal level as the Second Circuit Court of Appeals.

In order to understand both the horizontal and vertical relationship of courts, we need to know something about the organization of courts. Although there are rough similarities in the organization of courts from state to state, there are many more differences in detail than similarities. Many states, as well as the federal judicial system, now have three tiers or levels: (1) trial courts, (2) intermediate appellate courts, and (3) the court of last resort.

Trial courts and intermediate appellate courts usually have geographically limited jurisdictional boundaries. For example, there may be a trial court or courts for each county within a state, and each division or district of the intermediate appellate court will take appeals only from certain counties within the state. The court of last resort, i.e., the highest court within the jurisdiction, will usually have the power to review any decision from anywhere within the jurisdiction.

Unfortunately, the similarities end at this rather vague level of generality. The details, e.g., what courts are named, how the jurisdiction is divided territorially, and what courts have jurisdiction to decide what type of disputes, vary from jurisdiction to jurisdiction. In most states, the supreme court of the state (e.g., the Supreme Court of Illinois) is the court of last resort. But in some states, the court of last resort is given a different name. For example, in New York, the court of last resort is the New York Court of Appeals, and the Supreme Court of New York is the trial court. In the federal system, the intermediate appellate court is divided into circuit courts while in many states, the intermediate appellate court is divided into districts or divisions.

The diversity of trial courts is simply remarkable and defies systematic explanation. In any one state, you may see superior courts, municipal courts, justice of the peace courts, family courts, probate courts, juvenile courts, traffic courts, county courts, and small claims courts. Each state has developed its own peculiar set of trial courts.

The great diversity in our courts is primarily a result of historical development and haphazard, ad hoc planning over the years. The initial models of court organization in the United States were brought over from England. As will be seen, the English courts of the 1700's were organizationally complex and confused. Each colony (and, ultimately, each state) adopted its own version of the English system with slight variations in detail. Over time, these variations carried down through history.

To appreciate fully the modern organization of courts, we must trace some of this history. We begin in section B with the rough outlines of the English court system, especially its structure in the 1700's, when its influence over the American system was strongest.

In sections C and D we turn to the organization of the federal and state courts, respectively, and explain where you, the legal researcher, can find the work-product of those courts.

B. The English Court System

The single most important difference in the historical development of the English courts as compared with the historical development of American courts was the absence in England of a written constitution that established conclusively the jurisdiction and the power of the courts vis-a-vis the rest of government (which, in England, meant the King or Queen and Parliament, consisting of the House of Commons and the House of Lords). Instead of having their power expressly conferred and defined by a written constitution, courts in England have had power only to the extent that such power has been specifically granted by Parliament, by the King or Queen, or, during feudal times, by the feudal lords.

Because English courts were entirely the creation of the people in power at any one time, the developmental history of the English courts closely tracks England's development from a feudal system, with power decentralized in the hands of feudal lords with feudal manors, to a nation with power centralized around the King or Queen and Parliament, and then to a nation with power centralized almost exclusively around Parliament. And throughout England's history, its courts have always been subject, even in the resolution of individual cases, to control by the central government. Thus, the Upper House of Parliament (i.e., the House of Lords) early on arrogated to itself the power ultimately to review the decision of any court in any case. The House of Lords even today stands at the pinnacle of the English judicial system.

Once created by the government, a court itself becomes a center of power, and the history of English courts is thus also the history of individual courts expanding their jurisdictions and other courts outliving their usefulness but not disappearing. It has only been in the past 100 years or so that efforts were made in England to rationalize its system of courts.

1. The Common Law Courts

It is convenient to divide English courts of the 1700's into three basic categories: common law courts, equity courts, and specialized courts. As you will soon see, this division, though convenient, does not present a very accurate picture of the organization of courts in England since the ad hoc development of English courts led to the creation of many courts within each division that had overlapping and conflicting functions. But for our purposes, this division is sufficiently accurate to be useful, especially since this was the predominant view of the English system from the perspective of 18th century America.

Three courts emerged in England as central to the development of the common law: Common Pleas, King's Bench, and Exchequer. There were, to be sure, other courts in which civil or criminal wrongs could be rederessed; but these other courts did not have the same influence over the law that the three courts mentioned had. There was never a particularly clear jurisdictional difference between these three courts, and for years the courts battled amongst themselves for supremacy.

We need not be concerned here with the jurisdictional squabbles among these three common law courts. For our purposes, it is enough to know that each of these courts were limited in the type of cases they could hear and the type of relief they could award. The jurisdiction of a common law court could be invoked only on the basis of well-defined writs or forms. If a litigant could not fit his or her case within a pre-existing writ, no case could be brought.

As for remedies, the common law courts could award an injured person only "legal damages" to compensate the injured person for his or her loss. Damages include such things as out-of-pocket loss, loss of property, medical expenses, mental pain and suffering, and so forth. The common law courts generally did not claim for themselves the power of awarding injunctive or specific relief. Thus, for example, the remedy for a breach of contract was generally money damages rather than an order compelling the breaching party to perform the contract.

2. Equity Courts

It became apparent that great hardship could result from the limitation of the common law courts to legal relief (i.e., money damages). There were, after all, cases in which no award of money damages could reasonably be said to substitute for more specific relief. In response to the need in some cases for such additional relief, the English created another set of courts, the equity courts.

Originally, the equity court was nothing more than the Chancellor of England, the most important person in England after the King or Queen. Because of his position in the government, the Chancellor had extraordinary powers. Unlike the common law courts, whose jurisdiction was limited to specific writs and whose power was limited to awarding damages, the equity courts could grant specific relief against the defendant himself. Equity thus acted in personam ("against the person"), while common law courts acted only in rem ("against the defendant's property").

The two most important equitable remedies were specific performance (in which a party to a contract was ordered to perform the contract) and injunction (in which the defendant was ordered to do some act or refrain from doing some act). In both cases, noncompliance with the judgment of the Chancellor could result in an order of contempt and a jail sentence. It was this ultimate threat of jail that gave equity courts their real power.

3. Specialized Courts

In addition to the common law and chancery courts, there were created in England a number of specialized courts whose function was to handle cases involving specific subject matters. There were, for example, specialized courts to hear maritime and commercial disputes; county courts to hear civil matters involving petty sums; Courts of the Universities which had jurisdiction over personal actions and petty crimes involving university students; a Court of High Commission in Causes Ecclesiastical; Courts of Special Justices of Oyer and Terminer; and so on. It has been estimated that there were well over 100 separate courts in England at the time of colonization. Each of these courts developed special expertise and a distinct body of precedents.

The most important features of the English system for the development of American courts were the split between common law and equity and the existence of specialized courts. These features were adopted in one form or another in virtually all of the colonies, and this structure persisted in many states long after the Constitution.

In the 19th century, the law and equity courts were generally "merged," so that a single court could grant both legal relief (damages) and equity relief (specific performance and injunctions). This simplified one aspect of our judicial system. We have retained, however, the system of specialized courts both at the state and federal level.

C. The Federal Court System in the United States

1. Historical Overview

Because England lacked a written constitution setting forth the powers and responsibilities of the judicial system and separating the judicial system from the other branches of government, England never developed the clear separation of powers that exists in the United States. The absence of a written constitution meant that separation of powers in England was always a matter of tradition and practice. Particular kings or queens or runaway parliaments could abuse their power.

It was just such abuses of power that became the moving force to calls for independence in the American colonies. The Declaration of Independence is, more than anything, a catalogue of abuses that came about because, from the American perspective, all sovereign power was vested in an overseas monarch which did not allow colonial representation and participation in government.

Most of the complaints contained in the Declaration of Independence dealt with particular controversies between the colonies and England. Two complaints related particularly to the judicial system: "He has obstructed the administration of justice, by refusing his assent to laws for establishing judiciary powers. He has made judges dependent on his will alone, for the tenure of their offices, and the amount and payment of their salaries."

Following the American Revolution, the thirteen states agreed to form a confederation, and in 1778 they embodied that agreement in the Articles of Confederation. The salient feature of a confederation is the dilution of centralized power in favor of power concentrated in the individual states. The central government had relatively few powers and virtually no power to enforce any of its laws. There was no strong, central executive power, and no federal judiciary.

The Articles of Confederation proved unworkable in establishing a national government in large part because they reserved too many powers to the states and deprived Congress of the power it needed to operate effectively. A constitutional convention was convened in 1786, and led ultimately to the signing of the United States Constitution on September 17, 1787. The Constitution established a much more powerful federal government, but tried to insure against abuses of that power by splitting the sovereign powers between three co-ordinate branches of government: the legislative, the executive, and the judicial. We shall be concerned in the next few chapters with the structure and work of the judicial branch.

Article III of the Constitution is devoted to the establishment of the judicial branch of the United States. Section 1 of Article III provides that "[t]he judicial Power of the United States, shall be vested in one Supreme Court, and in such inferior Courts as the Congress may from time to time ordain and establish." By this language, the existence and jurisdiction of the Supreme Court of the United States is guaranteed. This was a partial response to the complaint in the Declaration of Independence that the King had obstructed justice by refusing to establish courts. The potential for abuse was not fully resolved, however, since inferior federal courts, such as the circuit courts of appeal and district courts, were to be created (and possibly destroyed) by act of Congress.

The independence of the judicial branch from the other branches is provided for primarily in Article III, Section 1 by the requirement that "[t]he Judges, both of the supreme and inferior Courts, shall hold their Offices during good Behaviour, and shall, at stated Times, receive for their Services, a Compensation, which shall not be diminished during their Continuance in Office." These provisions fully addressed the objection in the Declaration of Independence that judges were dependent upon the will of the King. The only method for removing a federal judge is impeachment by Congress, provided for in Article I, Section 3. Only 10 federal judges have been tried for impeachment, and of those tried, only 5 have been convicted. All of those judges were from inferior federal courts.

The Constitution established the Supreme Court of the United States and provided for the establishment of inferior federal courts. It also listed types of cases to which the federal judicial power could extend. The Constitution did not, however, expressly set forth the powers of the Supreme Court and lower federal courts vis-a-vis the federal legislature and executive, on the one hand, or the relation between the federal courts and the states, on the other hand. The Constitution thus left open two extremely difficult and important questions. First, to what extent, if any, may a federal court refuse to follow or declare void acts of Congress or the Executive that the court believes violate the Constitution? Second, to what extent, if any, does a decision by a federal court bind a state court in a later case, and to what extent does a decision by a state court bind a federal court?

The first question concerns the power of judicial review. The second question concerns issues of federalism.

a. Judicial Review

The Constitution did not provide for appeals from the Supreme Court to one or both houses of Congress, which would have been analogous to the English system. Instead, a clear separation of powers between the legislative and judicial branches was maintained. But there remained the question of whether the Supreme Court was obligated to apply whatever laws Congress enacted, or, instead, whether the Supreme Court was empowered to declare acts of Congress unconstitutional and to refuse to apply such acts. The judicial power to declare acts of Congress unconstitutional is called the power of "judicial review."

The issue of judicial review was addressed by the Supreme Court within only a few years of the Constitution's ratification. In *Marbury v. Madison*, 5 U.S. 137 (1803), the Supreme Court conclusively established the power of federal courts to declare acts of Congress unconstitutional. There has been relatively little dispute over the years concerning a federal court's power in this regard, although a few presidents and attorneys general have suggested that the Supreme Court's power is not as broad as is popularly believed. For example, President Abraham Lincoln's position was that, although the decisions of the Supreme Court bound the parties in a particular case, "the candid citizen must confess that if the policy of the government, upon vital questions, affecting the whole people, is to be irrevocably fixed by decisions of the Supreme Court, the instant they are made, in ordinary litigation between parties, in personal actions, the people will have ceased, to be their own rulers, having, to that extent, practically resigned their government, into the hands of that eminent tribunal." IV The Collected Works of Abraham Lincoln, p. 268 (Rutgers Univ. Press 1953) (First Inaugural Address, March 4, 1861). More recently, President Reagan's attorney general, Edwin Meese, made similar observations about the effect of Supreme Court decisions.

Despite these occasional objections, however, the Court's current view — and the view apparently accepted by most of society — is that the Supreme Court's decisions constitute the supreme law of the land and are generally binding. *See Cooper v. Aaron*, 258 U.S. 1 (1958).

b. Federalism

It is popularly believed, no doubt, that the Supreme Court of the United States, being the highest court in the land, has the power to review all aspects of any case tried in this country either in state or federal court. That is not true, however. The Supreme Court of the United States, and lower federal courts as well, declare what federal law is, but they do not finally determine what state law is. That function is entrusted to the highest court of each state, and a statement of a particular state's law by that state's highest court is binding even on the Supreme Court of the United States.

The Supreme Court of the United States will review such a determination of state law only for the very limited purpose of making sure that state law does not conflict with federal law or the United States Constitution. The Supreme Court will not even hear arguments in a case being appealed from the highest court of a state if the case involves only state law issues, on the ground that the state court's decision on state law matters is not reviewable by the Supreme Court of the United States.

Nothing in the Constitution requires that the Supreme Court's jurisdiction be limited in this way. The issue of whether it should be limited in this way raises questions about how our judicial system should work in the context of our federalist form of government (i.e., a government that has sovereign states which govern within certain territories and a federal government which governs all of the states). Another way of stating the question is whether the Constitution contemplated a unitary judicial system with the Supreme Court of the United States at its pinnacle, or whether the Constitution contemplated two judicial systems, one federal and one state, where federal and state issues could be raised in either system, and where the Supreme Court of the United States would review only federal issues. Through a gradual process of both legislative activity and judicial decisions, we developed into the latter type of system.

The fact that federal courts, including the Supreme Court of the United States, do not determine what state law is has an important influence on researching state law issues. When you research a state law issue, the most authoritative court is the highest court of the state whose law you are researching. A federal court's interpretation of a state's law, even the interpretation made by the Supreme Court of the United States, is only persuasive authority and is thus only evidence of what state law may be. *Fidelity Union Trust Co. v. Field*, 311 U.S. 169 (1940); *Erie Railroad Co. v. Tompkins*, 304 U.S. 64 (1938). You will learn much more about this topic in your course on Civil Procedure.

c. The General Structure of the Federal Court System

Although the Constitution provided expressly for the existence of the Supreme Court of the United States, because the Constitution did not specify the number of judges who would serve on the Court, their compensation, their method of appointment, or where it could meet, the Supreme Court of the United States did not formally convene until February, 1790, after Congress, in 1789, passed the first of many Judiciary Acts, 1 Stat. 73 (Sept. 24, 1789), and the first justices were appointed. The newly-created Court did not render its first decision until February of 1791.

The Judiciary Act of 1789 provided for a Supreme Court with a "chief justice and five associate justices." Judiciary Act of 1789, § 1. The Act also created thirteen districts and provided for a single district court within each district. *Id.*, §§ 2 & 3. The Act then divided the United States into three circuits, "the eastern, the middle, and the southern circuit." *Id.*, § 4. Justices of the Supreme Court were assigned to "ride circuit" in these three large areas when the Court itself was not in session.

From the very beginning, it was apparent that the Judiciary Act of 1789 was deficient in certain respects. These deficiencies may have been mere miscalculations. Professor Crosskey of the University of Chicago has argued, however, that the deficiencies were the intentional work of Jeffersonians who were engaged in a struggle to preserve States rights and undermine the ability of the federal government to regulate the conduct of the states. W. Crosskey, Politics and the Constitution, pp. 754–818 (Chicago Univ. Press 1953).

The primary deficiencies were in the jurisdiction granted to the lower federal courts and in the requirements of when and where federal courts could meet. The jurisdictional limitations prevented the district courts from hearing most ordinary cases brought by private citizens. The requirements of when and where federal courts could meet meant that even as to those cases where federal jurisdiction was present, it was very time consuming and expensive to get a case into federal court. The requirement that individual Supreme Court justices ride circuit tended to wear down the justices and make service in the federal judiciary less attractive.

The federal courts no longer operate under such artificial and debilitating limitations. Today, we have 95 district courts (the trial courts) within 13 federal circuits (the intermediate appellate courts). Appeals from final decisions of district courts are taken to the federal circuit in which the district court sits. Appeals from decisions of circuit courts are taken, usually by writ of certiorari, to the Supreme Court of the United States. The Supreme Court has discretion to grant or deny writs of certiorari, and the overwhelming majority (around 98% in recent years) are denied. It is now time to look at the work of these courts in greater detail.

2. The Supreme Court of the United States

a. United States Reports

The Supreme Court of the United States remains the single most important and watched court in this country. It should thus come as no surprise then that the decisions of that court are published in the greatest number of places and that those decisions are the most heavily indexed for researchers.

We begin with the official reporter for decisions of the Supreme Court of the United States. The official reporter was the only reporter until 1882, when the first unofficial reporter appeared. The official reporter for the Court's decisions is now titled United States Reports.

During the Court's first 85 years, it followed the English pattern of identifying case reports by the name of the person who edited and assembled the report. Thus, the first 4 volumes of what are now called the United States Reports may also be identified as volumes 1 through 4 of Dallas Reports. The next reporter was Mr. Cranch, and volumes 5-13 of U.S. Reports may also be referred to as 1-9 of Cranch. Here is a complete table of the early U.S. Reports and the parallel citation by reporter:

1789-1800	Dallas (1 Dall.)	1-4 U.S.
1801-1815	Cranch (1 Cranch)	5-13 U.S.
1816-1827	Wheaton (1 Wheat.)	14-25 U.S.
1828-1842	Peters (1 Pet.)	26-41 U.S.
1843-1860	Howard (1 How.)	42-65 U.S.
1861-1862	Black (1 Black)	66-67 U.S.
1863-1874	Wallace (1 Wall.)	68-90 U.S.
1875-date		91- U.S.

It is not necessary for you to memorize the names of these early reporters and the cross-reference to the U.S. cities. You do need to remember, especially when you read older cases, that prior to 1875, decisions of the Supreme Court were cited by reference to the reporter and not by reference to a U.S. volume. If you don't remember this fact, you might overlook citations to Supreme Court decisions simply because you don't see a "U.S." citation.

You should also be aware that Mr. Dallas reported decisions of both the Supreme Court of the United States and decisions from lower federal courts and from state courts in Pennsylvania. In fact, the first volume of Dallas contains no decisions from the Supreme Court of the United States. Don't be misled by the fact that the opinions appear in volume 1 of U.S. Reports.

Before reading further, you should get a volume of United States Reports. Please select one volume with volume number 400 or greater and then continue reading. Ask a librarian for help if you don't know where United States Reports is located in your library.

Turn to the title page of the volume you have chosen. The title page of a reporter almost invariably gives you a complete list of what the reporter contains. The title page of your volume indicates that it contains "Cases adjudged in the Supreme Court at October Term." The "October Term" lasts from the first Monday in October until around late June or early July of the following year. Thus, opinions from, for example, the 1971 term will include cases decided in the fall and winter of 1971 and cases decided in the spring and early summer of 1972.

The title page of your volume should also indicate the dates that the volume covers. The Court writes so many opinions of such length during the course of a term that the decisions of any one term are spread out over several volumes of United States Reports. The general pattern has been for the Court to dispose of relatively simple cases early on in the term and then to have a rush of important cases toward the end of the term. In recent years, the Court's output of opinions has varied from a low of around 85 cases to a high of around 125 cases.

As you can see on the title page, the job of Reporter of Decisions still exists, although we no longer refer to the reports by the name of the reporter. The Reporter in the Supreme Court releases opinions to the public and insures that opinions are properly assembled for printing by the Government Printing Office, which publishes United States Reports. The Reporter of Decisions also prepares a syllabus of Supreme Court decisions that is released along with the decision. The Supreme Court has held that the syllabus, which appears before the text of each opinion, is not part of the Court's opinion, and is intended only for the convenience of the reader. *United States v. Detroit Lumber Co.*, 200 U.S. 321, 337 (1906). You should never rely upon or cite a Supreme Court syllabus.

If you turn to the next page in your volume, you should see a list of Court personnel. The first names on the list are, as you might expect, the justices of the Court. Next come the names of living retired justices. This page also lists the names of certain officers of the Court: the Attorney General, who is the highest law enforcement officer in the Executive Department; the Solicitor General, who argues in the Supreme Court on behalf of the United States and, in certain important cases not involving the United States, at the invitation of the Court; the Clerk of the Court, who processes documents filed with the Court; the Reporter of Decisions, already described; the Marshal, who administers oaths when necessary and maintains order in the courtroom; and the Librarian, who oversees the Court's extremely large library.

If you turn a few more pages, you should come across a page that says near the top, "Allotment of Justices." Recall that Congress originally provided that individual justices would "ride circuit" and sit with the circuit court. Although justices no longer "ride circuit," each justice is appointed as "Circuit Justice" to oversee the activities of one or more circuit courts. The Allotment of Justices page indicates what assignments have been made. The primary function of a Circuit Justice today is to consider emergency petitions for relief from litigants who have first asked the circuit court for relief and have been refused. A single Supreme Court Justice (and emergency petitions are usually made initially to the appropriate Circuit Justice) has the power to stay the judgment of a lower court when necessary in the interests of justice. By far the greatest number of these petitions in the past twenty years have been made by prisoners asking for stays of execution pending review of their convictions and sentences by the Supreme Court.

The next few pages in the volume may contain special announcements by the Court during the term (e.g., the death or retirement of a justice, and the appointment of new justices). These pages may also contain, in a few volumes, rules promulgated by the Supreme Court that govern procedure in federal courts, such as the Federal Rules of Civil Procedure and Federal Rules of Evidence.

If you turn a few more pages, you should find the Table of Cases Reported. This contains a list of all opinions and orders of the Court reported in that volume. Turn to the beginning of the Table of Cases Reported and read the paragraphs at the top of that page. As the paragraphs indicate, the volume is divided into three sections. Opinions of the Court (which are opinions whose authorship is attributed to one or more justices) and decisions per curiam (which means an opinion "by the court" that is not attributed to any single justice), appear first in the volume. Next, appear cases in which no opinion was reported and only an order was entered. The vast majority of these decisions are orders refusing to hear appeals from decisions below or refusing to grant writs of certiorari. Finally, the last section contains opinions rendered in "chambers" by individual justices. These opinions are almost always opinions by a justice in his or her capacity as a Circuit Justice.

Opinions by the Court on federal questions, whether attributed to a single justice or per curiam are precedents for the Court itself and for all lower courts, both state and federal. Orders denying petitions for writs of certiorari have no precedential weight at all. Orders dismissing an appeal for lack of a federal question may have slightly more precedential weight, but are still generally not influential. On occasion, the Court will affirm a lower court judgment by order without issuing an opinion. These decisions — called summary affirmances — establish a precedent, but you must consult the lower court opinion to determine what the case was about. Opinions by a Circuit Justice have no significant precedential weight.

At this time you should glance at a few pages within each of the three sections just described to familiarize yourself with their general appearance.

Following the Table of Cases Reported is a Table of Cases Cited and a Table of Statutes Cited. These two tables indicate what cases and statutes have been cited in the reported decisions that appear in that volume. They are one type of index into the contents of that volume. They are not a useful index unless you know case names and statutes citations very well. A slightly better index, but still not a very helpful one, appears at the back of the volume. This index is prepared by the Reporter of Decisions and is an easy index to use so long as you know certain categories of constitutional claims (you will learn the right vocabulary in your course on Constitutional law). The index is still not particularly helpful for doing a research project because the index covers only the one volume, and your research must in almost all cases extend to all volumes of a reporter. This sort of an index is thus not helpful for doing a big research project; it is very helpful, however, for keeping up-to-date on a court's activity. When you are out in practice, you will not be able to read every opinion that the Supreme Court renders. The index allows you to cover very quickly the Court's work during the period of time covered by that index. As you will see, however, there are probably other research sources better suited to the task of keeping current on the Supreme Court's work.

Please return the volume you selected to the shelves for the next person to use (something you should always do unless contrary to your library's policy).

b. Supreme Court Reports — Lawyers' Edition

Lawyers Cooperative Publishing, a division of Thomson Legal Publishing Inc., publishes an unofficial reporter of Supreme Court decisions called United States Supreme Court Reports — Lawyers' Edition, now in its second series. It is more commonly known as simply the Lawyers' Edition. The first copy of Lawyers'

Edition appeared in 1882 and reported the decisions in volumes 1-4 of United States Reports. Lawyers' Edition contains all of the decisions of the Supreme Court of the United States.

You may be wondering why anyone would ever purchase an unofficial reporter rather than the official reporter. There are two reasons. First, unofficial reporters generally do more than just report court decisions. Most unofficial reporters are directly tied into other research aids published by the same company. Thus, your library typically would contain not only the unofficial reporter, but the other research aids that go along with that particular reporter. Second, unofficial reporters often are published more quickly than official reporters.

The Court has recently begun to computerize its publishing process, and there may be some reason to believe that the official reporter will be more current than it has been in the past. LEXIS and WESTLAW are unquestionably the quickest publishers of Supreme Court decisions. At present, Supreme Court decisions are available on these two systems usually within only a few hours of their release by the Supreme Court. You can thus read the full text of Supreme Court decisions before they are even reported on the evening news.

Go find Lawyers' Edition in your library (ask a librarian if you need help), and choose one of the volumes from the second series of Lawyers' Edition, volume 42 or above. You can easily identify the second series volumes because just below the volume number you will see "L. Ed. 2d;" volumes in the first series are labelled, by contrast, "L. Ed.". Don't continue reading until you have a volume from the second series in front of you.

Let's start again with the title page, just as we did with the U.S. reports. Just below the title and identification of which term the volume covers, you should see a line that says "Cases Contained in U.S. Reports." The next line then identifies what cases from United States Reports appear in this volume of Lawyers' Edition. Typically, one volume of Lawyers' Edition covers slightly more than one volume of United States Reports.

This cross-referencing to the official reporter is important because when you cite a Supreme Court decision to a court, you must use the official reporter citation (U.S.), if one exists. You may use an unofficial reporter citation only if the case has not yet been published in United States Reports.

If you look a little further down on the title page, you will see what the volume contains in addition to decisions of the Court. Volume 37 of Lawyers' Edition Second contains, for example, "Headnotes, Summaries of Decisions, Statements of Cases, Points and authorities of counsel, Annotations, Tables, and parallel References." None of these materials are contained in the official reporter.

You should now look at the next few pages in the volume. You will see many of the same types of pages that you saw in the official reporter. Generally, each page has a little more information than appeared in the official reporter to make you feel like you are getting something extra for your money.

Turn now to the beginning of an opinion somewhere in the middle of the volume. The first thing to notice is that just above the name of the case, you are given the parallel citation to U.S. Reports. That is the citation you must use when citing the case to a court. If you look just below the name of the case, you are given a citation that includes not only the parallel citation to U.S. Reports, but a parallel citation to another unofficial reporter, Supreme Court Reporter. More about Supreme Court Reporter later.

Lawyers' Edition then gives you a summary of the decision. The summary is prepared by the staff of Lawyers' Edition and, of course, cannot be cited to a court as part of the Supreme Court's decision.

Then Lawyers' Edition gives you a cross-reference to pages in the back of the volume where the Briefs of Counsel appear. The Briefs of Counsel are heavily edited versions of the briefs filed with the Court in the case. They can be extremely useful in understanding what arguments were made to the Court. The Supreme Court keeps unedited copies of all briefs filed with it, and Supreme Court briefs are also available on microfilm in many libraries and on WESTLAW and LEXIS.

The next thing in a Lawyers' Edition opinion is a list of Headnotes for that opinion. Just below the word Headnotes you should see a line that says "Classified to U.S. Supreme Court Digest, Annotated." A headnote is generally a note that appears at the beginning of an opinion (as opposed to a footnote, which appears at the bottom of a page, or an endnote, which appears at the end of a document). Headnotes printed before a court's opinion are generally drafted by the publisher of the reporter and not by the court, although a few courts still write their own headnotes. In any event, you cannot cite a headnote to a court as part of the decision of the court. It is the court's decision and opinion that controls, not the edited headnotes.

A headnote generally states a single rule of law that the publisher of the reporter thinks may be found in the court's opinion. Oftentimes, the language that appears in a headnote is simply a restatement of some of the court's own language. You can never be sure that a headnote correctly states the court's holding, however, since the publisher may have chosen the wrong language to cite, or there may be other language in the opinion that limits or qualifies the language picked up in one headnote. There is thus no substitute for actually reading the opinion.

Read headnote number 1 in the opinion you have before you. After you have read it, find the reference to headnote 1 in the opinion of the court. You should turn pages slowly and be looking for the following in bold at the beginning of one of the court's paragraphs: [1]. When you find that reference, read the paragraph in the text. You probably will find that some of the language in that paragraph appears in the headnote. Ask yourself whether you agree with the language chosen by the publisher for the headnote.

As already indicated, you should never rely exclusively upon a headnote when trying to figure out what a court's holding is. The headnote could be wrong. There is no substitute for reading the full opinion and applying your own skills of legal analysis to the problem.

You may be asking yourself, "then what good is the headnote if I can't rely upon it?" The answer to that question lies in the Digests. Headnotes are collected in digests. The headnotes in the Lawyers' Edition are collected in volumes known as U.S. Supreme Court Digest, Annotated. Every headnote in every volume of Lawyers' Edition appears in a volume of the accompanying Digest. The great value in Headnotes and Digests is that Digests are organized alphabetically by legal topic. Look again at headnote 1 in your opinion. Just before the number appears some language in bold-face type. There should be one or two words and then a section symbol ("§") followed by a number. Then a few more words. The first couple of words give you the Digest topic within the Supreme Court Digest. Using those words, you can locate the correct volume of Supreme Court Digest and the pages within that volume that contain the name topic. The section number then guides you to the correct pages within that topic. Under any one topic and section number, you may find a large number of headnotes.

The purpose of all of this is to organize and index the opinions of the Supreme Court by legal subject matter. If you can find a relevant topic within a digest and a relevant section number within that topic, you may be able to find cases relevant to your legal issue or fact situation. We will defer a more detailed discussion of digests until a subsequent chapter. Back to the Lawyers' Edition for now.

Somewhere in the middle of the headnotes, you should see a large box entitled "Total Client-Service Library References." This box contains cross references to other indexes published by the publisher of Lawyers' Edition. The first list references digest topics that are related to the legal issue decided in the case. The second list, under the title "Annotation References," references specific annotations appearing in prior volumes of Lawyers' Edition and in American Law Reports (you will learn more about American Law Reports and its annotations in chapter 5).

The final thing to note about opinions published in Lawyers' Edition is that the opinion indicates where page breaks occur in the official reporter. Thus, as you look through the opinion, you should periodically see something that looks like this: [422 U.S. 102]. These page cross-references are inserted by the publisher of Lawyers' Edition because of the general requirement that attorneys cite to the official reporter, U.S., rather than to an unofficial reporter. If you did not have these cross-references within Lawyers' Edition, you would have to subscribe not only to Lawyers' Edition, but also to the United States Reports. By including the cross-reference, the publisher of lawyers' Edition is giving you the option of subscribing only to Lawyers' Edition, saving you the cost of subscribing to U.S. Reports (or the inconvenience of using someone else's library to read U.S. Reports).

Turn now to the inside back cover of your volume. You should see there a pocket part. The pocket part, published every year, supplements the cases in the volume. Turn in the pocket part to the Publisher's Foreword and read it. As you see, the pocket part is designed to provide you with updated information about the cases reported in the volume. You should get used to checking every legal research source for pocket parts. It is a common method of updating the hard-bound volume.

c. Supreme Court Reporter

We now turn to the second major unofficial reporter for decisions of the Supreme Court of the United States: the Supreme Court Reporter. Supreme Court Reporter is published by West Publishing Company, the largest publisher of legal materials in the United States. The first volume of Supreme Court Reporter covers the 1882 October Term. Supreme Court Reporter does not contain any of the Court's earlier opinions, unlike Lawyers' Edition which contains all of the Supreme Court's opinions.

The Supreme Court Reporter, like Lawyers' Edition, is published more quickly than the official reporter. Softbound volumes are issued every two weeks or so while the Court is in session.

You should now retrieve from the shelves a volume of Supreme Court Reporter. As before, ask a librarian for help if you need it.

Let's go through our usual procedure. Turn to the title page and review what is contained in the volume. Note that one volume number of Supreme Court Reporter covers the Supreme Court's work for an entire term. Thus, for example, all decisions made during the 1981 October Term are reported in volume 102 of Supreme Court Reporter. Volume 102 is actually two books, 102 and 102A, but the page numbers in 102A pick up where volume 102 stops. Thus, 102A S. Ct. 3245 is an incorrect citation; the correct citation is 102 S. Ct. 3245.

Turn a few pages to the Table of Contents. The Table should contain things that are familiar to you from having looked at Lawyers' Edition: Justices of Supreme Court, Allotment of Justices, special orders, a cross-reference table to pages in United States reports, table of cases reported, and tables of statutes and rules cited.

The Supreme Court Reporter also contains a few things special to West publications. The first of these is a list of Words and Phrases. Turn to the pages listed for Words and Phrases. As you know from your other courses, many judicial decisions are resolved on the basis of interpreting a single word or phrase. The editors at West identify these legal terms of art and assemble them in alphabetical order in the multi-volume set Words and Phrases. The Words and Phrases pages in each Supreme Court Reporter show you what words and phrases the editors have identified in the decisions in that reporter.

Turn now to the beginning of an opinion in the volume. As you can see, West, like Lawyers' Edition, gives you parallel citations to the official reporter and the other unofficial reporter, Lawyers' Edition. Just below the name of the case and its docket number, you will see a short summary. That summary, like the summary in Lawyers' Edition, is prepared by the publisher and not by the Court. The summary will include citations to the decision below, if the decision was published. It will also indicate how the justices voted in the case and the disposition of the case (for example, whether the Court affirmed or reversed the lower court's decision).

Just after the summary comes the West headnotes. As with Lawyers' Edition, the headnotes are drafted by the publisher, and you can find the headnote references in the body of the opinion typically at the beginning of paragraphs. As with Lawyers' Edition headnotes, the West headnotes have a topic name and a number. Between the topic name and number you should see a key symbol. Because of that distinct key symbol, West's topic name and numbers are referred to as "key numbers." A complete "key number" consists of the topic name and the number that comes after the key. The key number plugs you into the West Digest System, undoubtedly the single most comprehensive index of decisions of United States courts, both state and federal.

Look at the first headnote in the opinion. Then turn to the back of the volume of the Supreme Court Reporter which contains the Key Number Digest for the decisions that appear in that particular volume (if you have selected a multi-book volume, i.e., volumes 102 and above, you will need to look in the back of the last book in the volume, e.g., volume 102A). You should be able to find the identical headnote under the appropriate topic name and number. Find that now. What you see in the Key Number Digest at the back of your volume is the same thing you will see in the complete volumes of the West Digest System. We will defer more detailed study of the West Digest System until a later chapter.

d. Other Supreme Court Reporters

The decisions of the Supreme Court of the United States are reported in a number of other places. Two widely used reporters are United States Law Week, published by the Bureau of National Affairs ("BNA") and Supreme Court Bulletin, published by the Commerce Clearing House ("CCH").

BNA's United States Law Week is part of a series of BNA publications that report on major developments in American law, both state and federal. The Supreme Court sections include, in addition to opinions of the Court, summaries of cases being appealed to the Court, summaries of petitions for writs of certiorari, summaries of important oral arguments, and periodic analysis of the work facing the Court during the remainder of the term. Law Week is published weekly and thus is an easy way to keep current with the Court's work.

CCH's Supreme Court Bulletin does pretty much the same thing as BNA's United States Law Week. Your choice between either of these is largely a matter of personal preference. In order to make an educated decision about which source to use, you should simply compare the two side-by-side.

The most current reports are now accessible only by computer. Both LEXIS and WESTLAW make Supreme Court opinions available the same day they are issued. Moreover, daily editions of BNA and CCH are also available on computer.

3. The Federal Circuit Courts

In the Judiciary Act of 1789, Congress created the first set of federal circuit courts. The original federal circuit courts were, in part, trial courts, and a trial could thus be heard in either the district court or the circuit court. An appeal from the decision of the federal circuit as trial court could be taken directly to the Supreme Court of the United States. An appeal from a district court generally could be taken to the circuit court.

As part of the effort to restrict the influence of federal courts in the United States, the Jeffersonians managed to provide in the Judiciary Act of 1789 that a circuit court could not act without the attendance of one Justice of the Supreme Court, and the circuit courts could meet at only very specific times in specific locations. The result of these limitations was that the federal courts oftentimes would not be sitting when a plaintiff needed to bring an action or, if they were scheduled to be sitting, could not sit owing to the absence of a Supreme Court justice. The state court system, being more complete and hospitable to the processing of claims, became the system of choice.

Ultimately, these restrictions were dropped, although the process was painfully slow, lasting over the next hundred years of our history. It was not until passage of the Judiciary Act of 1891 and the Judiciary Act of 1911 that the jurisdiction of the federal courts became established on a more even keel. These acts created the modern federal Circuit Court of Appeals and limited its jurisdiction to that of an appellate court. Appeals from district court decisions were taken to the circuit court. Appeals from circuit court decisions, in turn, went to the Supreme Court of the United States.

Prior to 1880, the decisions of the federal circuit courts and the district courts were not widely available and were not officially reported anywhere. The first volume of the Federal Reporter, published by West Publishing Co., appeared in 1880. The purpose of the Federal Reporter was to begin reporting in one place both oral and written decisions of the lower federal courts. The Federal Reporter was so popular that in only a few years, it became recognized as the official reporter for decisions by the lower federal courts.

The appearance of the Federal Reporter did not satisfy the profession's demand for information about federal decisions prior to 1880, and that demand resulted in 1894 in the publication by West of Federal Cases. Federal Cases is a 30-volume set of 18,313 decisions by the lower federal courts from 1789 to 1880. The cases are organized alphabetically by title, and all of the cases are digested in one volume at the end of the set.

By 1924, West had published 300 volumes of Federal Reporter. In November of that year, West continued its publication of lower federal court decisions in Federal Reporter, Second Series, which is commonly referred to by lawyers as "Fed Second" or "F. Second." Fed Second, like the Federal Reporter, contained decisions from both the circuit courts and district courts. In October 1932, the decisions of federal district courts began to be reported in a separate publication called Federal Supplement (discussed below). When that occurred, Fed Second stopped reporting district court decisions. Thus, beginning with volume 61 of F. Second, the only decisions that appear in F. Second are decisions of federal circuit courts of appeal, or other federal courts of similar stature (such as the Temporary Emergency Court of Appeals). F. Second ended in 1993 at volume 999, and F. Third began.

At this time, you should retrieve from the shelves a volume of Federal Reporter, Second. Please select a volume from 500 or above. Ask a librarian for help if you have difficulty finding Federal Reporters.

Turn to the title page. As you know by now, the title page generally tells you what courts' opinions are contained in the volume. As already indicated, Federal Reporter contains primarily the opinions of the United States Courts of Appeals, that is, the circuit courts. At one time or another, Congress has created special courts of appeals for special purposes (for example, the Temporary Emergency Court of Appeals), and the opinions of those courts may also be included in the volume you have selected.

Facing the title page is a map of the United States which shows the territorial jurisdiction of each federal circuit court. Congress has provided, as of today, for 13 circuits, the 11 numbered circuits, the D.C. Circuit and the Federal Circuit. *See* 28 U.S.C. § 41. You need to be aware of the individual circuits in your research. If you are in the Ninth Circuit Court of Appeals, for example, decisions of the Supreme Court of the United States are mandatory precedents and prior decisions of the Ninth Circuit Court of Appeals are treated as authoritative precedents. Decisions from other federal circuit courts are treated as only persuasive authority, however.

This treatment of the prior decisions of other circuit courts as only persuasive authority means that it is possible for two federal circuit courts to reach conflicting opinions on a single issue of law. The Supreme Court of the United States is of course able to resolve such conflicts, and a conflict between two circuits is a factor that weighs in favor of review by the Supreme Court of the United States. The Supreme Court of the United States does not always resolve such conflicts quickly, however. Indeed, the Supreme Court has allowed some clear conflicts to persist for many years.

There were not always 13 federal circuit courts. The Judiciary Act of 1789 created only 3 circuit courts, the eastern, middle, and southern circuits. The number of circuits increased because of the territorial expansion of the United States and because of the workload of particular circuits. This information is not simply cocktail small talk. Unless you are aware of this history, you can find yourself looking in the wrong place for cases or not looking somewhere that you should be looking.

The most recent example of the problems that can arise is the Fifth Circuit's split in 1981 into the Fifth Circuit and the Eleventh Circuit. The Eleventh Circuit, covering Alabama, Georgia and Florida, was created in 1981 by the Fifth Circuit Court of Appeals Reorganization Act of 1980, 94 Stat. 1994. Prior to its creation, those states were part of the Fifth Circuit. The Fifth Circuit was split into two circuits, the Fifth and Eleventh, because the workload of the Fifth Circuit had become too great for that Circuit to handle.

It was not administratively practical to create a new circuit out of thin air. There was instead a transition period when the Fifth Circuit was split internally into Division A and Division B. The Eleventh Circuit treats decisions from the old Fifth Circuit and Division B of the transition Fifth Circuit as decisions of the Eleventh Circuit. Therefore, if you are researching an issue in the Eleventh Circuit, you need to look not only for Eleventh Circuit decisions, but also for decisions by the old Fifth Circuit prior to its split and decisions by Division B of the transition Fifth Circuit.

The next page in the volume will be the Table of Contents. Review it quickly. Turn the page, and you will see the list of "Judges of the Federal Courts." This list gives you, by circuit, the names, appointment date, and location of each circuit justice, each Chief Judge of each circuit, all active circuit judges, all senior circuit judges, all active district judges, all senior district judges, and, at the end of the list, any special judges created by Congress.

Following the list of Judges is the list of Cases Reported for that volume. There are two lists of Cases Reported. The first list is arranged alphabetically by case name. The second list is arranged first by circuit and then, within each circuit, alphabetically. The circuit list of cases makes it easy for practitioners to read through the opinions from their circuit and, by so doing, to keep current on the law applicable in their jurisdiction.

Following the Cases Reported will be the usual sort of tables you have seen in the Supreme Court reporters concerning statutes and rules cited in the volume. There is no list of cases cited in the volume, as there was with Supreme Court reporters.

Turn now to the beginning of an opinion in your volume. It should look very familiar to you by now. You see the name of the case, the name of the court, the date the court decided the case, a West synopsis of the case, West key number headnotes, the names of the attorneys who worked on the case, the names of the judges, and the opinion of the court.

Turn back now to the list of Cases Reported and find a case name that has the word "(Table)" after the case name. Then turn to that page in the volume. You should see on that page a long list of case names, numbers, dates, and a disposition for the case (e.g., "AFFIRMED", "REVERSED"). This table is the list of "Decisions Without Published Opinions." Turn to the beginning of the list and you will see which circuit court's unpublished opinions are being listed. Each circuit has its own local rule about publishing opinions, but the general approach taken is that cases that may easily be decided upon prior precedent and present no interesting factual or legal questions may be decided without a published opinion. In some circuits, between 40-50% of their opinions each year are unpublished. Generally, an unpublished opinion may not be cited as precedent in any court. The only thing you may cite is the disposition in that particular case (i.e., you may cite the lower court opinion, if any, and indicate that it was affirmed or reversed on appeal).

4. The Federal District Courts

We come now to consider the work of the federal district courts, which are the federal courts of first instance or trial courts. It is in the district court that complaints are filed and trials occur. This is where the vast bulk of judicial work is done in the federal system.

Selected opinions of federal district courts are published in the Federal Supplement. You must be aware, however, that not every case decided in the federal district court results in a written opinion that is reported. In fact, the vast majority of cases do not result in a published opinion. Indeed, some federal district judges as a matter of practice publish none of their opinions. They view their job not as publishing opinions and making law but as deciding individual cases on the basis of binding precedent.

As already indicated above, decisions of the federal district courts prior to 1880 can be found in Federal Cases and decisions of those courts between 1880 and 1932 can be found in Federal Reporter and the first 60 volumes of Federal Reporter, Second Series. In November 1932, West began publishing the Federal Supplement. Federal Supplement was created because the number of cases coming from both the circuit and district courts had reached such a level that West could justify publishing the decisions in separate volumes. There is not yet a second series.

You should locate a volume of Federal Supplement from the shelves. Ask a librarian for help if you have difficulty locating the Federal Supplement reporters.

Follow the procedure we have established in this chapter for reviewing a new case reporter. You will discover that Federal Supplement is set up in much the same way as Federal Reporter, which is no surprise since both are published by West Publishing Company.

5. Other Reporters of Federal Decisions

You now have been introduced to the three main official sources of common law as it appears in the federal courts: United States Reports, Federal Reporter, and Federal Supplement. These are not, however, the only sources for finding the opinions and decisions of federal courts. For example, West publishes a set of volumes known as Federal Rules Decisions ("F.R.D.") that contains decisions from federal district courts concerning the Federal Rules of Civil Procedure and Federal Rules of Criminal Procedure. West also publishes a Bankruptcy Reporter ("Bankr.") that contains decisions from all federal courts, including the Supreme Court, in bankruptcy matters.

In addition to these West reporters, there are quite a few other reporters that contain federal decisions relating to a specific area or areas of law (e.g., tax, antitrust, trademark, copyright, labor, and so forth). The two largest publishers of these materials, which are typically in the form of ring binders and loose-leafs, are BNA, the Bureau of National Affairs, and CCH, the Commerce Clearing House. These topical reporters are of value primarily to practitioners who specialize in particular fields of law.

6. Citation Form for Federal Reporters

When you include citations to sources in a legal document, you should expect that the reader may desire to examine the sources cited. It is therefore important that your citations contain sufficient information so that a reader may find the material you have cited. Furthermore, because the universe of legal sources is so diverse, it is generally a good idea for all lawyers to agree roughly upon citation form. Agreement as to the content and form of legal citations simplifies the job of finding cited material.

There is no formal agreement as to citation form. Different jurisdictions have established different traditions. The most widely used citation manual is A Uniform System of Citation, Fifteenth Edition (1991), more commonly known as the Blue Book because it often (although not always) is published with a blue cover. The following summary of federal case citations is taken from the inside front cover and Rule 10 of the Blue Book.

A proper citation to a decision published in the United States Reports includes the name of the case (with appropriate abbreviations), the volume number, the report identifier ("U.S."), the page number, and the year of the decision. For example, *Erie Railroad Co. v. Tompkins*, 304 U.S. 64 (1938). If you are citing to a dissenting or concurring opinion, you should also include a parenthetical identifying the author of the opinion. For example, *Raymond Motor Transportation, Inc. v. Rice*, 434 U.S. 429, 449 (1978) (Blackmun, J., concurring). If the decision has not yet been reported in U.S., you may cite to any of the unofficial reporters, with L. Ed. 2d or S. Ct. preferred, if available.

Citations to lower federal opinions are only slightly different. Because Federal Reporter and Federal Supplement include cases from many different courts, you need to include in your citation the identity of the court. For example, a citation to *United States v. McPartlin*, 595 F.2d 1321 (1979), is incomplete because the citation does not identify which circuit court decided the case. The proper form is *United States v. McPartlin*, 595 F.2d 1321 (7th Cir. 1979). The same rule applies to district court opinions in F. Supp. You do not need to include the name of the Supreme Court in a U.S. citation because the identity of the court is obvious from the reporter identifier (e.g., 434 U.S. 429).

Lower court decisions may have a subsequent history on appeal (such as affirmed or reversed). You will learn later in this chapter how to find such subsequent history. For now, you should know that any important subsequent history should be added to your citation. Thus, for example, if the Supreme Court denied a writ of certiorari, that subsequent history must be included: *United States v. McPartlin*, 595 F.2d 1321 (7th Cir.), *cert. denied*, 444 U.S. 833 (1979). Consult rule 10.7 in the Blue Book for a list of subsequent history phrases.

D. The State Court Systems

1. Historical Overview

You will recall from our review of the organization of English courts two main features: the primacy of Parliament and the ad hoc development of specific courts. These two characteristics were carried over in one form or another in all 13 of the original colonies. The legislative and executive departments retained the power of reviewing judicial decisions in individual cases. As for the creation of specific courts, the colonies generally followed the broad structure of English courts, but not its intricate detail. Early on, the equity side was generally nothing more than an appeal to the governor of the colony sitting as a judge of equity. But by the time of the American Revolution, there had come into being a true equity court in most states. This division was to last in most states for well over one hundred years. Today, all states have merged their equity and common law courts. There is now one set of judges that handle both equitable and common law matters.

The state court system, like the federal court system, has become increasingly systematized since the signing of the Constitution. For example, all states now have a trial court of general jurisdiction from which appeals may be taken to either an intermediate appellate court or, in some states, directly to the highest court in the state (often known as the supreme court of the state but sometimes given a different name, such as the New York Court of Appeals). Unlike the federal system, however, state court systems have retained the old English practice of having a large number of specialized courts to handle particular grievances. All states thus have a large number of other specialized courts to deal with particular subject matters (e.g., traffic court, family court, small claims court, and so on). We will not be concerned with these specialized courts in these materials, since the decisions of these courts are almost never published anywhere.

2. Courts in California

We now consider in slightly greater detail the materials currently available in the State of California. What you will see in California is similar to what can be seen in many other states. Some states do not have the same number of unofficial reporters as California does; some states, however, like New York, have a similarly rich choice of reporters from which to choose.

There are three basic sources for California decisions: the official reporters (California Reports and California Appellate Reports); an unofficial reporter for the state (West's California Reporter); and the unofficial regional reporter (for California, West's Pacific Reporter). We treat these three reporters in sequence.

a. Official State Reports

The official reporter for decisions by the Supreme Court of California is California Reports, which is now in its fourth series. Volume 1 of the first series of California Reports contains the decisions and opinions of the Supreme Court of California for 1850, the first term of that court. California Reports is structured very much like the United States Reports which we have already considered. Each volume contains a table of cases, tables of statutes and rules cited, headnotes for each case, a summary drafted for convenience of the reader, and so forth.

Decisions of the intermediate appellate courts in California were not officially reported until 1905 with the appearance of California Appellate Reports, also now in its fourth series. We thus have a complete record of appellate decisions in California only from 1905 onward.

b. Unofficial State Reporters

Beginning in 1959, West Publishing Co. has reported California cases in an unofficial reporter titled California Reporter. This unofficial reporter, now in its second series, contains in a single set all of the decisions published in the two official reporters from 1959 to the present. Since California Reporter is a West publication, the headnotes are tied to the West Digest System. West publishes an unofficial reporter for New York called the New York Supplement, now in its second series.

c. Unofficial Regional Reporters

Decisions of California courts prior to 1959 and many decisions since then are also reported in the volumes of Pacific Reporter, now in its second series. Pacific

Reporter is one of the West Regional Reporters that is part of the West National Reporter System. The reporters in the National Reporter System are as follows:

Atlantic Reporter (A. or A.2d)

Connecticut, Delaware, Maine, Maryland, New Hampshire, New Jersey, Pennsylvania, Rhode Island, Vermont, and the District of Columbia

North Eastern Reporter (N.E. or N.E.2d)

Illinois, Indiana, Massachusetts, New York, and Ohio

North Western Reporter (N.W. or N.W.2d)

Iowa, Michigan, Minnesota, Nebraska, North Dakota, South Dakota, and Wisconsin

Pacific Reporter (P. or P.2d)

Alaska, Arizona, California, Colorado, Hawaii, Idaho, Kansas, Montana, Nevada, New Mexico, Oklahoma, Oregon, Utah, Washington, and Wyoming

South Eastern Reporter (S.E. or S.E.2d)

Georgia, North Carolina, South Carolina, Virginia, and West Virginia

South Western Reporter (S.W. or S.W.2d)

Arkansas, Kentucky, Missouri, Indian Territories, Tennessee, and Texas

The National Reporter System was begun in 1883 and has become the single most comprehensive source of state decisions in this country. It includes all decisions from the highest court of every state from the date of initial publication. Each case contains the West key number headnotes and is digested in the accompanying American Digest System. You will learn more about that system in a later chapter.

For state cases prior to the 1880's, you must resort to the volumes of American Decisions and American Cases. These volumes represent as close an approximation as possible to a complete report of decisions in the several states from 1658 to 1896.

3. Citation Form for State Reporters

Citations of state decisions are similar in form to citations of federal decisions. Each citation must include the name of the case, the volume number, the reporter identifier, the page number, a court identifier (if that is not obvious from the reporter identifier), the year of decision, and any subsequent history. The major difference between federal and state citations is that you at times must include a parallel citation for state decisions, if available, particularly when writing briefs or memos for courts within the state whose cases you are citing. Thus, for example, in writing for a California court, the proper citation form for a Supreme Court of California decision is as follows: *J'Aire Corp. v. Gregory*, 24 Cal. 3d 799, 598 P.2d 60, 157 Cal. Rptr. 407 (1979). If, however, you are writing for a New Jersey court and are citing the California case, the citation could appear as 598 P.2d 60 (Cal. 1979). In all situations, of course, you should check the rules governing a specific court to assure that you meet that court's citation requirements. *See* Blue Book Rule 10.3.1.

E. Updating Cases

Probably the single most serious error that a legal researcher can make is the failure properly to update the initial results of research. It would be far better not to find a case at all than to find the case, rely upon it, and only later discover that the decision had been overruled by a higher court. You must update all research.

We will identify in these materials several specific methods of updating particular legal sources. For sources not covered in these materials, you will have to learn on your own how to update your research. Most legal sources contain a section explaining their use — a "How To Use This Book" section — and that section will often explain how to update your research in that source. It is a good idea whenever you use a source for the first time to review the "How to Use" section to make sure you are making the best possible use of the source.

The primary method of updating cases is to use the Shepard's Citations system, available both in book form and on LEXIS and WESTLAW. The many hard-bound volumes and soft-bound supplements of Shepard's Citations are published by Shepard's/McGraw-Hill Inc. In general terms, Shepard's is used to update the law as it is found in a single case, the "root" case, by listing all subsequent cases that have cited the root case.

For example, suppose you need to update *Basso v. Miller*, 40 N.Y.2d 233, 352 N.E.2d 868, 386 N.Y.S.2d 564 (1976), to determine whether the law stated in that opinion concerning a landowner's duties to a trespasser is still the law in New York. Using Shepard's, you can find every subsequent decision that has cited *Basso*. Since *Basso* is a leading decision on the topic from the highest court in New York, you can be pretty sure that *Basso* will be cited by any court faced with issues similar to the issues raised in *Basso*. You can be doubly sure that the New York Court of Appeals would have cited *Basso* in any case involving duties owed to trespasser. Thus, because Shepard's gives you the citations to all subsequent decisions that have cited *Basso*, you can easily and quickly update the law as stated in *Basso*.

Shepardizing cases is a mechanical task. All you need in order to Shepardize are three pieces of information: (a) the volume number of the case; (b) the name of the case reporter; and (c) the page number of the case. For *Basso*, you have (a) volume 352, (b) N.E.2d, and (c) page 868 (or, alternatively, (a) volume 40, (b) N.Y.2d, and (c) page 233).

The Shepard's system is divided up by case reporters. There are different Shepard's volumes for every case reporter. For example, there is a United States Shepard's that is used to Shepardize U.S. citations; there is a Supreme Court Reporter Shepard's for S. Ct.; and, there is a Lawyers' Edition, Second Series, Shepard's for L. Ed. 2d.

For *Basso*, 352 N.E.2d 868, you would select the Shepard's volumes for North Eastern, Second Series. If you went to the library to find this set of volumes, you would probably discover that there are four hard-bound volumes. The first covers 1 N.E. to 51 N.E.2d; the second (which supplements the first) covers 1 N.E. to 200 N.E., which is the last volume in N.E.; the third covers 1 N.E.2d to 305 N.E.2d (which replaces the first volume with respect to 1 N.E.2d to 51 N.E.2d); and the fourth (which supplements the third) covers 1 N.E.2d to 425 N.E.2d. There are, in addition, two soft-bound supplements (a Gold and Red supplement).

In order to Shepardize *Basso*, 352 N.E.2d 868, you would use the hardbound volume for 1 N.E.2d to 425 N.E.2d and both supplements. As you can see, Shepardizing by hand can be a somewhat tedious process.

Each book in Shepard's contains hundreds or thousands of pages of citations. Once you have found the correct books of Shepard's (that is, the ones that cover the case reporter for the case you want to Shepardize), the next step is to locate in those books the volume and page number of your case. You should retrieve a volume of Shepard's from the shelves and follow along.

Each page in Shepard's contains all three pieces of information that you need to Shepardize. The volume number for the beginning of the page (or for the end of the page) is printed in the upper-left hand corner (or the upper-right hand corner), and the beginning of each new volume is clearly marked in the columns (you may have to turn a few pages to see the bold "Vol. #" text). The name of the reporter is clearly marked at the top of each page. Finally, the page numbers appear in each column (e.g., "-868-"). The citations below the page number indicate cases that have cited the case you are Shepardizing. The citations are in an abbreviated form to save space. A table of reporter abbreviations appears in the front of every Shepard's volume.

Once you have Shepardized a case using the appropriate hard-bound Shepard's, you need to update that research by looking in the Gold, Red, and, if one exists, White (or coverless) supplements. The procedure for finding the case is the same in the supplements. Find the supplement for the correct reporter and then find the volume and page numbers of your case within that supplement.

WARNING: Because the supplements come out so regularly and frequently, if you cannot find the Gold and Red supplements, it is probably because someone else is using them and not because they do not exist. Not all Shepard's have a White (coverless) supplement, but you need to be aware of the possible existence of a White supplement. If you have any question about whether a particular supplement exists, it is a very good idea to check with your librarian.

In addition to giving you citations to all cases that have cited the case you are Shepardizing, Shepard's gives you the parallel citation for the case. Parallel citations are indicated in Shepard's by a cite contained in parentheses just below the page number for the case you are Shepardizing. Look around a few pages until you see a cite within a parentheses. That will be a parallel citation.

Shepard's also gives you information about the subsequent history, if any, of a case (such as whether it was reversed or affirmed or whether a cert petition was denied), and information about how the case has been treated by subsequent opinions (such as whether it was followed or distinguished). This information is conveyed in the letters that sometimes appear next to citations in Shepard's. Glance at a few pages in Shepard's, and you should see these letters every now and then (e.g., "a", "j", "s", "f" and so forth). A table of these letters appears in the front of every Shepard's volume. For obvious reasons, it is particularly important that you learn the meaning of some of these letters: "a" (affirmed), "r" (reversed), "v" (vacated), "m" (modified), "s" (superseded), and "o" (overruled).

Even though the Shepard's supplements are frequently published, Shepard's will be several months behind the work of the courts. One solution to this problem is to use LEXIS or WESTLAW to update your research, which will be discussed in the next chapter. Ultimately, in order to be completely up-to-date, you must as an attorney keep yourself generally aware, by consulting daily or weekly legal newspapers, of the work of your own courts.

(Matthew Bender & Co., Inc.)   (Pub. 776)

CHAPTER 3

COMPUTER-ASSISTED LEGAL RESEARCH

A. Introduction to Computer-Assisted Legal Research

Modern information and communications technologies have fundamentally altered the way in which we interact with each other and with the world. Virtually no aspect of life has been immune from these technological inventions. The practice of law and the process of legal research have been similarly transformed.

That the practice of law would be transformed as a result of modern information technologies should have come as no surprise to anyone. Lawyers and courts spend most of their time processing information. And legal research is essentially the process of locating and collecting relevant information.

The most salient characteristic of the information and computer revolution is the dramatic reduction in the cost of storing and manipulating information electronically as compared with the cost of storing and manipulating information printed on paper. The initial purchase of a computer with memory may represent a significant expenditure, and there are certainly ongoing costs of maintenance and upkeep. But once the computer is in place and up and running, the actual costs of manipulating information within the computer is trivial (e.g., the cost of the electricity necessary to keep the computer turned on).

The computer revolution has represented something of a challenge to book publishers, who have sunk millions of dollars into printing technologies that in the computer age are increasingly becoming obsolescent. As a result, legal book publishers have been somewhat reluctant to embrace publication of materials in a computerized format when sales of computerized information apparently reduces sales of books. Happily, there have been just enough publishers willing to forge ahead with computerized publications to exert competitive pressure upon all publishers, and we are beginning to see a steady flow of new computer-based legal publications.

The computer market moves so quickly that it is nearly impossible to keep up with new products. This book will introduce you to two of the oldest, most complete systems of computer-assisted legal resarch, LEXIS and WESTLAW. There are many other computer-assisted legal research systems now available, many of which rely upon the new CD-ROM technology. Although there are differences in the details of how each of these systems operates, many of them are patterned upon LEXIS and WESTLAW, and competence on these two systems will go a long way to making you generally competent to perform computer-assisted legal research on any other system.

B. Introduction to LEXIS and WESTLAW

LEXIS is a product and service of Mead Data Central Corp., although that is about to change with the recently announced sale of LEXIS by Mead Data to Reed Elsevier. LEXIS was developed in the 1970's and began widely appearing in law schools and law offices in the early 1980's. WESTLAW, a product and service of West Publishing, was developed nearly contemporaneously.

Both systems operate in basically the same way, although their appearance on the screen (i.e., their look and feel) is substantially different. The two companies try to differentiate their competing systems by the scope and completeness of their coverage and by offering differing pricing structures. In law school, you will not be worried about the cost differences, but in practice, the costs of operating the two systems will probably be an important factor in influencing your choice.

At bottom, both systems perform the same basic research functions. First, you can search through the actual, complete text of legal sources (e.g., cases, statutes, secondary sources) by entering in "queries" or "search terms," and both systems will then display (or print or down-load to your computer) the text of all documents which satisfy your request. Second, you can update most authorities using an on-line version of Shepard's as well as special electronic updating services available on both systems.

On WESTLAW — and this is one of the few big differences between the two systems — cases come complete with the West syllabus and West digest headnotes. This means that nearly all of the West digest system is available for your use as a searching aid on WESTLAW.

Those of you who have had significant computer exposure will be especially tempted by the theoretic prospect that all of your legal research could be performed by computer. After all, not only can you use the computer to find the relevant authorities, but you also can have the computer print out the cases just as they might appear in a reporter (complete with two columns).

This is a temptation that you must resist for several compelling reasons. First, the simple matter of cost. As a student, you will not notice the expense of using LEXIS and WESTLAW, and it is very much in their interest to hook you as a student so that you will continue to use their systems as a practicing lawyer (and paying customer). While some research functions are more efficiently performed by computer (i.e., they cost less for the same return), many research functions can be performed more cheaply without the "aid" of a computer. As just one simple example, if your law firm already has a complete set of reporters, it might not be be cost-effective to print out individual cases from LEXIS and WESTLAW. When you enter practice, the cost of legal research — a cost which you and your firm will attempt to recoup from clients — becomes a more important issue.

Second, some research tasks — particularly research in secondary sources and digests — are probably better done using the books. Secondary sources and digests come with topical indexes and tables of contents that help organize the material (and organize your thinking). There is, in other words, a great deal of intelligence built into these sources. By contrast, when you perform a word search on LEXIS or

WESTLAW, the computer mechanically looks for exactly the words you have specified — there is no intelligence built into the machine. As a result of this difference, relevant cases and authorities that could be missed on the computer are more likely to be found in the secondary sources and digests.

Third, it is not possible at present conveniently to browse through sources on LEXIS and WESTLAW. Browsing through secondary sources is often a good way of becoming familiar with a field of law, and many a research problem has been solved "inadvertently" as a result of stumbling across relevant sections in secondary sources.

There are, of course, certain types of research that are performed much more efficiently by computer, and a few types of research that can be performed only by computer. For example, you will discover that the computerized version of Shepard's is much easier to use, making it much less likely that you would make a mistake in updating your authorities. LEXIS and WESTLAW are also excellent for performing very narrowly focused research where you can be relatively certain about the exact language which would appear in relevant documents. For example, if you were going to be drafting an appellate brief for an intermediate appellate court, you could easily find all opinions published by each of the three judges before whom you were scheduled to appear by searching for the names of those judges in the appropriate LEXIS or WESTLAW database. This type of research could not be conveniently performed by hand.

When all is said and done, you will have to develop for yourself a judgment about the most efficient research strategies to solve particular problems. Law school is the time to experiment, when a client's interests are not on the line. You are strongly encouraged in law school not to focus all of your research efforts on either the books or the computers. A competent researcher uses all available sources.

C.   Selecting Databases On LEXIS and WESTLAW

The first step in performing a search of documents on LEXIS and WESTLAW is to specify the set of documents that you want to search. Both systems have so many documents available that it would be prohibitively expensive to search every document on the system with every search. More importantly, you will usually want to limit your searches to specific jurisdictions and types of documents. If you are litigating in Texas, for example, you probably will want to focus most of your attention upon Texas state court decisions and, secondarily, decisions from the federal district courts in Texas and the U.S. Court of Appeals for the Fifth Circuit (which includes Texas within its geographic jurisdiction). Most of the time, you probably will want to exclude cases from other state's courts (cases which would be only persuasive authority in Texas). Similarly, if you are searching for relevant statutory or administrative materials, you may want to exclude court decisions from your search initially.

After signing on to LEXIS or WESTLAW — and you should feel free at this point to pick a system and continue reading while actually using one of the systems — you will see a page containing what amounts to a table of contents for databases on the system. On LEXIS, this first page contains what LEXIS chooses to call

"Libraries"; on WESTLAW, this first page simply has page numbers for different categories of databases (such as federal cases, state cases, federal statutes, and so forth). If you are on LEXIS, type the name of a Library (such as "genfed") and press ENTER; if you are on WESTLAW, type a page number (such as "p4" for federal cases) and press ENTER.

The next page you will see contains the names of specific databases that you can select (on LEXIS, databases are called "files"). You select a database simply by typing in its name and pressing ENTER. As you might expect, the database categories generally follow the existing jurisdictional lines between courts. If you have selected "genfed" on LEXIS or "p4" on WESTLAW, you should see a list of databases for federal judicial decisions, and you should select the database for decisions of the Supreme Court of the United States (i.e., "US" on LEXIS and "SCT" on WESTLAW). That's all it takes to select a database.

It will not be obvious only from the name and description of the database exactly what documents are included in particular databases. For example, if you selected the SCT database on WESTLAW, you would not have in that database all of the decisions from the United States Supreme Court. You would have decisions from 1945 until the present, and you would need to select a different database to retrieve the older decisions.

In order to determine the actual scope of a database, you need to ask for it specifically. On LEXIS, just before selecting a FILE, you can enter a page number for each FILE for a description of its scope. On WESTLAW, you can request the scope of a database by typing "scope" (instead of typing a search request) and pressing ENTER.

You will often want to change databases (don't do it now, though, because the search example in the next section begins with a search for Supreme Court decisions). For example, if a search limited to Supreme Court decisions doesn't pan out, you may want to search decisions from federal appellate courts. To change to a new database on LEXIS, you simply press the "CHG FILE" or "CHG LIBRARY" key (or ENTER ".cf" or ".cl"). LEXIS will then take you back to the pages which display FILES or LIBRARIES. To change to a new database on WESTLAW, type "db" and press ENTER (which will then display the table of contents for databases), or if you know the name of the database you want to change to, type "db [database name]" and press ENTER (e.g., "db cta2" to change to the database for the Second Circuit Court of Appeals).

D. Performing Searches on LEXIS and WESTLAW

If you have been following along on LEXIS or WESTLAW, you will have selected decisions from the United States Supreme Court as your database, and you will now be on a page that invites you to enter your search terms (LEXIS calls this a "search request," and WESTLAW calls it a "query").

1. Searching for the "Good Search"

The ability to formulate a good search is a sophisticated talent that you will develop only through hours of thought and practice. Both LEXIS and WESTLAW will find all documents within the selected database that satisfy your search terms. A "good search" cannot be defined in terms of whether the computers find the documents you have asked for; you can be confident that the computers will find exactly what you have asked for.

A "good search" has to be defined, instead, as a search which finds documents relevant to your ultimate research objectives. If your search terms miss too many relevant documents, your research may be incomplete (since LEXIS and WESTLAW obviously cannot report on documents not found, you will not even know that you have missed the relevant cases!). On the other hand, if your search terms find too many documents, some of which are relevant but many of which are not relevant, you may again end up with incomplete research. For example, if your search finds 1,000 cases, and the thirty or so relevant cases are buried in that pile, you are unlikely to spend the time reading through all 1,000 cases, and you will then miss the relevant ones that are hidden underneath the irrelevant ones.

A "good search" then is one which finds most or all of the relevant documents and does not find very many irrelevant documents. To restate the matter slightly, you are hoping for a search that properly discriminates between relevant and irrelevant documents and produces a high yield of relevant documents.

2. Formulating Basic Searches

Searches on both LEXIS and WESTLAW consist of words, logical connectors, and proximity operators. In the best of circumstances, you hope that by creatively combining words with logical connectors and proximity operators, your search will find documents that contain refrences to concepts relevant to your research objective. The important thing to remember, however, is that LEXIS and WESTLAW will not be searching for concepts; instead, the systems will mechanically be searching for exactly what you have specified in your search request. Enough theory. The best way to learn how well the systems work is to try them out.

a. Words

A search request consisting of a single word is the simplest type of search request. For example, if you were to search for the word [homosexual] in the SCT database on WESTLAW, you would discover that only 50 or so Supreme Court opinions contain the word "homosexual" (in these materials, sample search requests will be enclosed within brackets — when you type in the search request on LEXIS or WESTLAW, do not type the brackets). If you were doing research on the question of whether it is a denial of equal protection for the government to discriminate on the basis of sexual orientation, finding all Supreme Court cases mentioning homosexuality is one way of approaching your research. And since your search request discovered only 50 or so cases, you could plausibly read or browse through all of them.

If you are on LEXIS or WESTLAW, go ahead and type in [homosexual] and press ENTER. The next screen will show you the first page of the first case found by this search. Let's assume that you don't have the time to read through all 50 or so cases, and that you would like to try to narrow your search to a subset of those cases. In order to edit your search request, press the "new search" key on LEXIS (or type ".ns" and press ENTER), or type "q" and press ENTER on WESTLAW. That should take you back to a screen which will permit you to edit your search request.

Searching for a single word will usually produce far too many cases, and, in particular, far too many irrelevant cases. For example, suppose you wanted to research the question of whether a gun control statute was constitutional. Searching for the word [gun] in the SCT database on WESTLAW would produce over 350 cases. Unless you have a lot of time to spend (and your client has a lot of money to burn), that is too many cases conveniently to review, particularly since the word "gun" is likely to appear in many cases having nothing to do with gun control (e.g., it would appear in many criminal cases where a gun was used in the commission of a crime). That is why most of your search requests will include multiple words connected by logical connectors and proximity operators.

There are just a few other details about words on LEXIS and WESTLAW. First, both systems search for regular plural versions of words (e.g., a search for [gun] would find cases using the plural "guns"). WESTLAW also searches automatically for certain irregular plurals (e.g., [woman] will also search for "women").

Second, certain words on both systems are considered non-searchable because they appear too often. For example, the words "a" and "the" are not searchable.

Third, both systems employ the same two special universal characters, "*" and "!", to permit you to find different variants of a root word. The exclamation point may appear only at the end of a word, and it instructs the computer to find all documents containing words that begin with the root word, no matter how long the words are. For example, a search for [negligen!] would find documents containing the words "negligent", "negligence", and "negligently" (as well as any others words that begin with "negligen"). If you make the root word too short (e.g., [neg!]), it probably will recover far too many words, so use as many letters in the root word as you can.

The asterisk is a limited universal character. As shown in the example above, the exclamation point is indifferent to the number of characters after the root word. The asterisk, by contrast, will match only those words that contain the same number of extra letters as there are asterisks. For example, [negligen*] would find "negligent", but it would not find "negligence" or "negligently". And [negligen**] would find "negligence", but it would not find "negligent" or "negligently". The asterisk, unlike the exclamation point, can be used within a word in cases when there may be an alternative spelling or you want to search for different tenses (e.g., [gr*w] would find both "grow" and "grew").

b. Logical Connectors

Both systems use the same logical operators, "or" and "and", to connect words. These logical connectors work pretty much as you would expect. If your search request is [homosexual or gay], the system will find all documents containing either the word "homosexual" or the word "gay", or both words. If your search request is [homosexual and gay], the system will find all documents containing both the word "homosexual" and the word "gay".

The "or" connector is most useful when the concept you are searching for can be expressed using a variety of different words. If you wanted to find cases involving boats, for example, you might want to include in your search request [boat or ship or vessel]. The "or" connector always expands your search request.

The "and" connector is used to limit your search request to those documents which contain both words. Many concepts are expressed using phrases, and many legal rules use multiple terms of art. The "and" connector is helpful in these circumstances. In other situations, you will want to find cases that apply a particular legal doctrine to a particular fact situation. The "and" connector is also helpful here. For example, as explained above, if you searched Supreme Court decisions for the word [homosexual], you would find 50 or so cases. Suppose you wanted further to limit your search to cases in which the Court discussed both homosexuality and the doctrine of equal protection. You could do this by entering the following search request: [homosexual and equal and protection]. Performing this search would reduce the number of cases found from around 50 to around 20. That would appear to be a much more tailored search request (remember, of course, the warning above that a search can become too narrow and can exclude relevant cases).

In some cases, you may want to exclude cases that contain certain words. Both systems have a logical connector to permit you to perform this function, although LEXIS and WESTLAW unfortunately use different connectors. On LEXIS, you can use the "and not" connector to exclude documents. On WESTLAW, you can use the "but not" or "%" connector to exclude documents. For example, if you searched on LEXIS for [battery but not criminal], LEXIS would find all cases that contain the word "battery" but would then exclude any case containing the word "criminal" (you might perform this search in order to find cases involving the tort of battery without finding all of the criminal cases involving battery). The "but not" and "and not" connectors are especially dangerous because you will deliberately be excluding cases from your search results, thereby increasing the risk that you will miss relevant cases. Use these connectors with caution and intelligence.

c. Proximity Operators

You probably noticed above that it was rather awkward to search for [homosexual and equal and protection] since the words equal protection will very likely be used by a court as a phrase when the court is trying to refer to the doctrine of equal protection. Both LEXIS and WESTLAW have special operators to let you search for words which are located close to each other in the document. These are called proximity operators.

On WESTLAW, when you want to find a set of words that are located right next to each other (e.g., the words in a phrase), you can enclose those words between quotation marks. To find the phrase equal protection, for example, you would use a search request of ["equal protection"], and in our example above, you could combine that phrase with the word "homosexual" as follows: [homosexual and "equal protection"]. If you do not use the quotation marks, the search will not work since WESTLAW interprets spaces that are not within quotation marks as "or". Thus, [homosexual and equal protection] would be searched by WESTLAW as though you had entered [homosexual and equal or protection].

On LEXIS, when you want to find a phrase, you can just type in the phrase without quotation marks. So on LEXIS, a search for the phrase equal protection would be entered simply as [equal protection].

LEXIS and WESTLAW also permit you to find words that are located a specified number of words away from each other by using the "w/#" proximity operator where # is a number. For example, if you wanted to find cases where the issue discussed by the court was whether noise from a neighboring property was a nuisance, you could search for [noise w/10 nuisance]. This search will find all documents in which the word "noise" is within 10 words (either before or after) the word "nuisance".

The two systems do this search in a slightiy different way. In performing this search, LEXIS counts only searchable words between the words you have specified; WESTLAW counts all words between the words you have specified.

If you want to limit you search to cases in which the word "noise" appears before the word "nuisance", you can use the "pre/#" operator on LEXIS ([noise pre/10 nuisance]) and the "+#" operator on WESTLAW ([noise +10 nuisance]).

WESTLAW, but not LEXIS, has two more proximity operators that permit you to locate documents in which words are used within sentences, "/s" and "+s", and within paragraphs, "/p" and "+p". The slash ("/") version of these will find documents in which both words appear somewhere in the same sentence or paragraph irrespective of their order. For example, [peace /s mind] would find documents containing either the sentence "her peace of mind was upset" or the sentence "her mind was set at peace". The plus ("+") version requires that the first word appear before the second word. Thus, [peace +s mind] would match only the sentence "her peace of mind was upset". The sentence and paragraph proximity operators are particularly useful since, unlike the numerical proximity operators, they are based upon natural breaks within documents, breaks that may identify whether the document actually discusses the two words together.

d. Order of Processing

Finally, we must discuss the order in which LEXIS and WESTLAW process these connectors and operators. Neither system processes search requests simply from left to right. Although you may think this unnecessarily complicates matters, both systems correctly assume that you actually do not want your request processed from left to right.

An example will make the point. Suppose you wanted to locate documents involving negligent driving of a car, but you recognized that courts often use the word automobile instead of car. You might type in the following search request: [negligen! and car or automobile]. If the systems processed this left to right, they would end up finding documents which contained either (1) both the words "negligent" and "car", or (2) the word "automobile". In other words, the systems would treat the search request as though it was grouped as follows: [(negligen! and car) or automobile].

Both systems use the same order of precedence, which is as follows:

(1) phrases

(2) or

(3) proximity operators

(4) and

(5) and not / but not

Because of this order of precedence, in the search request [negligen! and car or automobile], "car or automobile" will be grouped together first (since "or" is processed before "and"), and "negligen!" will be added next. In other words, the search request would be treated as though it said [negligenc! and (car or automobile)].

If you want to override the order of precedence or simply make it clear to the systems what you want (particularly if you don't remember the order of precedence), you can actually use parentheses just as shown above to group your search terms in any way that you wish.

e. Searching Segments or Fields

Documents on both LEXIS and WESTLAW are divided into smaller units called segments on LEXIS and fields on WESTLAW. For example, the name or title of a case is located in the "name" segment on LEXIS and in the "title" field on WESTLAW. You can search individual segments or fields simply by typing the name of the segment or field and then enclosing search terms inside of parentheses. For example, to find *Roe v. Wade* in the Supreme Court database, you could search for [name(Roe and Wade)] on LEXIS and [title(Roe and Wade)] on WESTLAW.

You can get an online list of the segments or fields by pressing the "segmts" key on LEXIS or entering only the word "fields" on WESTLAW. It is a good idea to familiarize yourself with the available segments or fields, and if you are following along on one of the systems, you should take a moment now to examine the online listing.

One of the most commonly used segments or fields contains the date of the decision. Both systems let you limit your search to cases decided before a specified date, exactly on a specified date, or after a specified date. Date restrictions on WESTLAW are added at the end of a search request with an "and" connector, and look like this:

```
and date (bef March 15, 1993)   (cases before the date)
and date (3/15/93)              (cases on the date)
and date (aft 3-15-93)          (cases after the date)
```

The format is slightly different on LEXIS. LEXIS does not expect the specified date to be located within parentheses. So the same searches on LEXIS would be typed in as follows:

```
and date bef 3/15/93            (cases before the date)
and date is March 15, 1993      (cases on the date)
and date aft 3-15-93            (cases after the date)
```

3. Reading the Documents

Once the systems have completed a search, they will display any documents which have been found. Reading documents is relatively easy on both systems, and both systems permit you to browse portions of documents to speed up your review process.

The two most common methods of reading on the systems are to read the full-text and to read only those portions of the text which are located near your search terms. To read full-text on LEXIS, you should press the "full" key (or type ".fu" and press ENTER) when reading a case. The full-text of the document will be displayed, and you then move forward or backward by pressing the "next page" or "previous page" keys (or type ".np" or ".pp" and press ENTER).

To read full-text on WESTLAW, enter the letter "p" while reading a document, and WESTLAW will then display the document in "page mode". To move forward on WESTLAW in page mode, you can just press the ENTER key. To move backward or to skip to any page within the document, ENTER "p#" where # is the page number to which you want to skip.

To browse the portions of the document near your search terms on LEXIS, you can press the "kwic" key (or ENTER ".kw"), which stands for Key Words In Context. You can then move forward or backward through the document with the "next page" and "previous page" keys, and LEXIS will display only those portions of the document near your search terms.

On WESTLAW, you perform the same function by selecting the "term mode". WESTLAW automatically puts you in the "term mode" when it first reports the found documents. If you change to page mode (by entering "p"), you can change back to term mode by typing "t" and pressing ENTER. When you are in term mode, simply pressing ENTER will move you forward through the documents.

Your search requests usually will find more than one document, and there are keys and commands to let you move between documents. On LEXIS, you use the "next doc" or "previous doc" keys (or type ".nd" or ".pd" and press ENTER). On WESTLAW, documents are given rank numbers beginning with 1, and you ENTER an "r" to move forward by one document, or ENTER an "r#" where the # is the document number you want to skip to.

Finally, both systems permit you to review the citations of all documents found by your search. On LEXIS, just press the "cite" key (or type ".ci" and press ENTER). On WESTLAW, type "l" (which stands for "list") and press ENTER.

You will need to practice all of these functions to become familiar with them. After an hour or so, you won't even need to think about what keys to press since it will quickly become second nature to you.

E. Updating Authorities on LEXIS and WESTLAW

The last topic in your introduction to computer-assisted legal research is updating authorities on LEXIS and WESTLAW. You will be happy to learn that most of the volumes of Shepard's that you will be using are available on both LEXIS and

WESTLAW, and that Shepardizing cases on these systems is as simple as typing in the correct case citation. There is no need on these systems to consult multiple volumes. Although there are some differences in the way Shepard's is displayed on the two systems, the differences are generally at the level of detail; functionally, both systems do the same thing.

There are only a few important warnings about Shepard's on LEXIS and WESTLAW. Unfortunately, not all volumes of Shepard's have been added to the computers. For example, Shepardizing 4 U.S. 1 on LEXIS produces only citations after 1943. The Shepard's display indicates its "COVERAGE" on the first page, and you should always check the coverage to make sure you have all of the citations. If the coverage is less than complete, you will need to use the printed volumes of Shepard's.

Second, you must remember that Shepard's online is no more current than the printed supplements. Shepard's sends out its printed supplements at the same time that it releases citations for LEXIS and WESTLAW. As described below, there are other ways to be more current than Shepard's on LEXIS and WESTLAW.

In order to access Shepard's on LEXIS, you can press the "shep" key (or type ".sh" and press ENTER). On WESTLAW, just type "sh" and press ENTER. If you are on one of the systems now, try Shepardizing *Basso v. Miller*, 40 N.Y.2d 233, 352 N.E.2d 868, 386 N.Y.S.2d 564 (1976). On LEXIS, you need to press "shep" and then type in one of the citations. On WESTLAW, you can type "sh 352 N.E.2d 868" and press ENTER. When you are done with Shepard's and want to leave, press the "resume" key on LEXIS, or type "gb" (which stands for "go back") and press ENTER on WESTLAW.

There is one additional way of updating case authority that brings you up to within five days of the receipt by publishers of case information. LEXIS has the Auto-Cite service (press the Auto-Cite key) to perform this function, and WESTLAW has the Insta-Cite service (type "ic" and press ENTER) to perform the same function. As with Shepard's, all you need do is type a case citation. Unlike Shepard's, Auto-Cite and Insta-Cite do not give you every citation to the specified case. But both systems give you specific information about the history of the case and its precedential value. For example, they will tell you whether that particular decision was affirmed, reversed or modified, and whether it has been expressly overruled, by subsequent decisions. This information will be critically important to you in confirming that the cases you have found are the most recent cases and still represent good law.

F. Signing Off

To sign off of LEXIS, you simply press the Sign Off key (or type ".so" and press ENTER). To leave WESTLAW, you type "off" and press ENTER.

This chapter has been introductory only, and while a few references will be made to LEXIS and WESTLAW throughout the remainder of this book, there is an enormous amount of information about these systems that is not covered here. You are encouraged to read the reference manuals published by LEXIS and WESTLAW, to talk to your fellow students about their experiences, to ask help from your media or reference librarian, and to take advantage of any special training classes offered by LEXIS and WESTLAW representatives.

CHAPTER 4

LEGAL DIGESTS

A. Introduction

In Chapter 2, you were introduced to the structure of American courts and the books that contain the reported decisions of those courts. In order to read any particular case, all you need is a volume number, a reporter name, and a page number. With those three things, the common law is open for your consideration.

The problem in doing legal research, of course, is to find citations to the relevant cases. That is the problem we shall be addressing in the next two chapters: How do you find decisions that are relevant to a particular legal issue or fact situation you have been instructed to research? Asked more simply, how do you find your way into the cases?

In this chapter and the next, we shall be concerned primarily with researching state law contract and tort issues. Although our focus will be on state courts and on only two substantive areas (contracts and torts), the research techniques we will cover can be used equally well in federal court and in other substantive areas.

B. The Problem

Assume now and for the remainder of this chapter that Ms. Smith (Partner) has given you (Associate) the following assignment:

> "One of our clients, Perfect Pipes Inc., submitted a bid to a general contractor on a city project. Because of a clerical error, the bid submitted was for $5,700 rather than for $7,500. The next highest bid was at $7,250, and the general contractor used Perfect Pipes' bid in making his bid to the city. The general contractor was awarded the contract. Our client wants relief from his mistake. California law applies. I seem to remember a case, *Drennan v. Star Paving*, 51 Cal. 2d 409, 333 P.2d 757, where the California Supreme Court held that the general contractor was entitled to rely even on a mistaken bid, and the sub-contractor was therefore bound. I want to know whether that case is still good law in California and, more generally, what the law in California is about relief from mistaken bids."

C. Analysis of the Problem

When you receive a research assignment, you should not simply run off to the library and begin opening books. You should first answer for yourself two questions: (1) what exactly am I being asked to do (or, phrased differently, what is the scope of the research problem)? (2) What is the best way to conduct the research requested?

Ms. Smith has asked you to do two things: (a) update *Drennan v. Star Paving* and (b) find out what California law provides with respect to mistaken bids by sub-contractors. The first task may quickly be accomplished by Shepardizing *Drennan*, which you learned how to do in Chapter 2. In addition to determining whether *Drennan* has been overruled or modified, you are likely to find through Shepard's nearly every mistaken bid case in California, since *Drennan* was a leading case.

Your research would not be complete, however. Even though *Drennan* is a leading case, there might be a few California cases subsequent to *Drennan* that deal with the legal issue of unilateral mistake but do not cite *Drennan*. Shepard's would not lead you to these cases. That brings us to the subject of this chapter, West's American Digest System.

D. An Overview of the Legal Digests

Because our common law system is built upon the idea of following precedents and because the practice of law is a business as well as a profession, it is vital to be able quickly to find relevant cases. One of the most efficient finding tools is a legal digest, and the most comprehensive set of digests is published by West, the West Digest System.

A digest is a collection of short case annotations organized by legal issue. Because the annotations are organized by legal issue, it is possible to find in one place citations to cases that deal with one legal issue. Because the digest itself contains an index and table of contents, it is relatively easy to locate the annotations that deal with specific legal issues.

For example, if you needed to find cases setting forth the legal test for what constitutes an "offer," you would simply look in the index to the West Digest under "contracts — offer." The index would then direct you to a particular volume and page in the Digest system where you would find all cases that define "offers."

During the first hundred or so years of our country, no one published a widely accepted digest of the cases. Indeed, the cases themselves were only sporadically reported. The confusion generated by this state of affairs led ultimately in about 1850 to the creation of the 8-volume set "United States Digest," the first digest of American cases. The Digest had the almost magical property at the time of allowing any lawyer to find most of the cases relevant to an issue appearing in the digest system, and the United States digest was quite popular with lawyers and courts.

As you know from Chapter 2, West began its National Reporter System in 1879 and contemporaneously published all prior American cases in American Decisions. At the same time, West was hard at work creating its own Digest System that would be tied in directly to its National Reporter System.

A case published by West contains headnotes written by West editors. Each headnote states a single rule of law that the editors believe appears in the decision. These headnotes are then categorized by topic and number, and each headnote is added to the West Digest System under its assigned topic and number. A topic and number in the West Digest system is known as a "key number." The headnotes are then assembled by the assigned key number and published in the West Digest System.

The first annual digest from West, the American Annual Digest, appeared in 1887. The American Annual Digest was much easier to use than the United States Digest, and it also was more complete in its coverage. The United States Digest could not withstand the competition, and the final volume of United States Digest was published only one year later.

Within ten years, West had completed its larger project of creating a digest for all American cases. In 1897, West published the Century Digest, a 50-volume set encompassing all American cases decided between 1658 to 1896. That amounted to something around 500,000 cases.

West continued to compile new digests as cases around the country were decided, and every ten years, West issued a new set of volumes covering cases decided from all state jurisdictions during the preceding ten years. There are now 10 sets of these Decennial Digests, each one covering a ten-year span (the Ninth and Tenth Decennial Digests are divided into Parts 1 and 2, each covering a five-year period (only Part 1 for the Tenth, covering 1986-1991 has been published as of the date of this writing).

During the years between Decennial Digests, West publishes a General Digest. Because of the large number of cases being decided by our courts, there are a correspondingly large number of General Digest volumes. As of November 1994, for example, there are 44 volumes of General Digests covering the years 1991-1994. By the end of the the current five-year period (1996), there will be over 50 volumes of General Digests.

The Decennial and General Digests are not very convenient because of the large number of volumes and because they contain cases from all American jurisdictions. In order to do complete research using the Decennial and General Digests, you would need to look in all ten of the Decennial Digests (the first nine decennials and part one of the tenth decennial) plus the 44 volumes of the General Digests. In practice, it will be a relatively rare research problem that will require you to go through this time-consuming process (and a rare client who can afford it).

Typically, you will know what state's law applies, and you will be most interested in the law of that state. It is for that reason that West has also divided its Digest system by geographic region and by court. In particular, West publishes a series of five regional digests that are tied into the seven regional reporters (there is no digest for the North Eastern Reporter or the South Western Reporter), and West also publishes individual state digests for all states except Nevada and Delaware, as well as a separate digest for the federal courts. In addition to state decisions, the state digests include references to decisions from federal courts within the state. The headnote and key numbers in these regional and jurisdictional digests are identical with what is published at about the same time in the Decennial and General Digests. West adds new key numbers every now and then as the need arises. The following table lists the books available in the West Digest System:

Century Edition	All Cases, 1658-1896
Decennial Digests	All Cases, 1896-1986
General Digests	1986-

U.S. Supreme Court Digest	Supreme Court Only
Federal Digest	All Federal Courts, 1754-1938
Federal Practice Digest	All Federal Courts, 1939-1961
Federal Practice Digest, 2d	All Federal Courts, 1961-1975
Federal Practice Digest, 3d	All Federal Courts, 1975-
Bankruptcy Digest	Bankruptcy Reporter
Military Justice Digest	Military Justice Reporter
U.S. Court of Claims Digest	U.S. Claim's Court Reporter
Atlantic Digest	A.
Atlantic Digest, 2d	A.2d
North Western Digest	N.W.
North Western Digest, 2d	N.W.2d
Pacific Digest	P.
Pacific Digest, 2d	P.2d
South Eastern Digest	S.E.
South Eastern Digest, 2d	S.E.2d
Southern Digest	So.
State Digests	All except Nev. & Del.

The first step in doing digest research is to select the correct digest. Ms. Smith wanted to know about the law of mistake in California. There are three digests that you could use, the Decennial and General Digests, the Pacific Digest (2d), or the California Digest, now in its 2d series. The Decennial and General Digests are too inconvenient.

The Pacific Digest includes many cases outside of California and, probably more important, does not include decisions from federal courts within California. Thus, if you use Pacific Digest, you would probably need to check the Federal Practice Digest for California federal cases which, although not formally precedents in California, are sometimes very persuasive within California and are often a good source for finding citations to California cases. The best choice is the California Digest, 2d, since it includes all California state cases as well as decisions from federal courts within California.

As you can see, even the seemingly simple question of picking the right set of digest volumes requires some sophistication. You are strongly encouraged to examine the different sets of digest volumes that encompass your state to determine what set gives you the best coverage of relevant cases.

E. Finding Key Numbers in the Digest System

The West Digest System is organized around the "key number." A key number in the West Digest System is made up of a topic name and a number (e.g., "Assignments 33" is the key number that deals with "Agreements to assign"). Each West headnote is given a key number. Each headnote is then included in the West Digest System under its assigned key number. Thus, if you can find a relevant key number, you can find relevant cases.

There are three basic ways of finding relevant key numbers: (1) Find a case that has a relevant key number without using the Digest System (e.g., you may already know one case dealing with the issue you are researching); (2) Use the General Index to the appropriate Digest; and (3) Use the Table of Contents of a particular Topic within the Digest (e.g., if you know you have a contract issue, simply scan the table of contents for the "Contracts" topic).

1. The Case Approach

One approach to finding a relevant West key number is to find a relevant decision published in a West reporter using some other research source. As you know from Chapter 2, each decision published in a West reporter contains headnotes drafted by West editors. Each headnote is then given a key number within the West Digest System. Thus, if you can find a relevant case, you can use the key numbers in the headnotes for that case to begin your research in the West Digest System.

In the problem given to you by Ms. Smith above, she identified for you *Drennan v. Star Paving*, 51 Cal. 2d 409, 333 P.2d 757 (1958), as a relevant case. If you were to consult the West reporter, 333 P.2d 757, you would discover that headnotes 9 and 10 of the case relate to the issue of mistake, and those headnotes have been given key number Contracts 93(1). That is where you could begin your West Digest research.

2. The General Index Approach

The last few volumes in every set of West Digests contain a General Index. The index contains entries for many legal concepts (e.g., consideration, res ipsa loquitur) and entries for commonly occurring facts (e.g., automobiles). You may thus find it useful in using the index to break your research problem down into its legal components and its factual components. The index may contain entries for both.

For example, Ms. Smith's research problem involves the legal issues of "mistake" in "contracts" in the factual context of "bids." If you were to consult the entry for "contracts — mistake" in the California Digest, Second, you would discover that it instructs you to "see this Index, Mistake." Consulting "mistake," you would discover two possibly relevant entries. First, you would see "mistake — bids for municipal contract. Mun Corp 332, 354." Second, you would see "mistake — contracts — generally. Contracts 93." This gives you several possibly relevant key numbers: Mun Corp 332, Mun Corp 354, and Contracts 93.

3. The Table of Contents Approach

The other most common method of finding a West key number is to review the Table of Contents that appears at the beginning of each West topic. For example, Ms. Smith's assignment relates generally to the field of "contracts." Reviewing the table of contents for this topic, you would quickly discover the listing for "93. Mistake," which would again give you the right place to start your research.

The Table of Contents approach works well if you are relatively familiar with the area of law being researched and are therefore likely to recognize the legal shorthand that appears in the Table of Contents. If you are not familiar with a particular area of law, the Table of Contents is likely not to be very informative.

If you are unfamiliar with a field of law, it is a good idea to begin your research with other secondary sources, discussed in the next chapter, before consulting the West Digest. Proper use of the West Digest requires a familiarity with the subject matter.

F. Updating The West Digest

Once you have found the right key number, you can look in the hard-bound volume to find all headnotes and cases under that key number. That will give you a list of possibly relevant cases. For example, if you were to examine the California Digest, Second, for the Contracts 93 keynumber, you would discover a series of cases, including *Drennan v. Star Paving*, dealing with the topic of mistake.

But your research at that point will be limited to cases decided prior to the date of publication of that volume. West provides two types of supplements to update your research. First, each volume contains a "pocket part" which is located on the inside of the back cover of each volume. The pocket part contains headnotes from recent cases. You must always check for a pocket part to insure that you have the most recent cases. Second, for many of the digests, a cumulative supplement is published updating all of the volumes from the dates of the most recent pocket part. The cumulative supplement is usually a paper-bound volume(s) physically located just after the index volumes (at least that is where many librarians put it). You must always check the cumulative supplement, if one exists, to insure that you have the most recent cases.

When you have your list of case citations from the main volume, pocket part, and cumulative supplement, you are ready to go read the cases to determine which cases are actually relevant to your research assignment. You should never rely solely upon a West headnote in deciding whether a case is relevant. You must read the case yourself. When you have read the cases and discarded the irrelevant ones, you then are ready to update those cases with Shepard's.

G. The West Digest on WESTLAW

As you would expect, WESTLAW takes advantage of the West digest system. The opinions on WESTLAW include both the West syllabus and all of the West headnotes. Each headnote is given a unique keynumber so that you can search for keynumbers on WESTLAW. A keynumber in the printed digests is made up of a topic name and a section number (e.g., Contracts 93). On WESTLAW, the topic names have been given numbers. A list of the numbers is available on WESTLAW by selecting database "key" (i.e., typing "db key" and pressing ENTER).

You should try to do Ms. Smith's research assignment on WESTLAW. After you sign on, select the "key" database and find out what the number is for topic "contracts". Then select the California database for state decisions and search for that keynumber. The search will consist of the topic number, the letter "k", and the number 93 (e.g., [3k93], although 3 is not the right number). Give it a try and see how it works. You can then perform the same search in database "allcases" which will search nationwide. See how many cases you get.

CHAPTER 5

SECONDARY SOURCES

A. Introduction

We continue in this chapter with an examination of sources for citations to relevant cases. Chapter 4 was devoted to the Digest System. This chapter is devoted to a variety of other secondary sources that contain citations to and discussions of cases and the common law. We shall review in this chapter legal encyclopedias, restatements of the law, treatises, law review articles, legal dictionaries, and casebooks.

B. The Problem

Assume now and for the remainder of this Chapter that Ms. Smith (Partner) has given you (Associate) the following assignment:

> "Our client is a land-owner who is the defendant in a personal injury action. The plaintiff, an adult, fell through a trap door in our client's barn. The plaintiff was trespassing at the time but was not engaged in any criminal conduct. Plaintiff alleges that our client negligently maintained the trap door. New York law applies. I seem to remember that the New York Court of Appeals held in *Basso v. Miller*, 352 N.E.2d 868, that a land-owner owes a duty of reasonable care even to a trespasser. I want you to find out whether *Basso* is still good law in New York and what the law generally is around the country. Don't give me every decision around the country; I just need an overview."

C. Analysis of the Problem

As in Chapter 4, you should first analyze the problem to determine the exact scope of the assignment and the best research strategy to complete the assignment. You are being asked to do two things: (a) Update New York law to determine whether the rule stated in *Basso* is still the law of New York; and (b) Determine at a general level (without citations to "every decision around the country") whether the rule adopted in *Basso* is generally accepted in other states and, if not, what rule is accepted.

The first task, updating New York law, you do by Shepardizing *Basso* and by checking the New York Digest to find all cases involving a landowner's duty to a trespasser. You could do the second task, review the law around the country, using the Decennial and General Digests. As indicated in Chapter 4, however, those sources are relatively inconvenient to use. You also could look in all of the regional digests. That, of course, involves looking in many volumes, and there is no regional digest for the North Eastern Reporter and South Western Reporter.

An important limitation on the assignment given was that Ms. Smith does not want "every decision" on the issue; she only wants an overview. In this Chapter, we identify other secondary sources that can be used for this sort of general background research: legal encyclopedias, American Law Reports, Annotated, the restatements of law, treatises, law reviews, and casebooks.

D. Legal Encyclopedias

1. Corpus Juris Secundum (C.J.S.) and American Jurisprudence (Am. Jur.)

An encyclopedia is "[a] comprehensive reference work containing articles on a wide range of subjects or on numerous aspects of a particular field, usually arranged alphabetically," American Heritage Dictionary, p. 452 (2d College Ed. 1982). The two leading legal encyclopedias are Corpus Juris Secundum (C.J.S.), published by West Publishing Company, and American Jurisprudence, published by Lawyers Cooperative/Bancroft-Whitney and now in its second edition (Am.Jur.2d).

There are quite a few similarities between these two sources. Both are multivolume sets; both are divided into broad subject matter headings (e.g., Contracts, Torts, Civil Procedure); both are divided within the subject matter headings into sections discussing discrete legal issues; both contain case citations in footnotes; both purport to state generally recognized principles of law; both are updated with pocket parts.

There are a few differences between C.J.S. and Am. Jur., however. C.J.S. purports to cite all relevant cases in its footnotes while Am. Jur. purports to cite only a sample of leading cases. For your purposes as a legal researcher, this difference is probably more apparent than real. You could never rely upon C.J.S. as a final source; no matter what you find in C.J.S., you will want to update the research with a Digest and Shepard's. Thus, so long as Am. Jur. has a citation to a case within your jurisdiction, you are on your way. Furthermore, if your research is limited to finding general principles, Am. Jur. does that job essentially as well as C.J.S. Nevertheless, if you are using an encyclopedia as a tool for finding cases rather than for learning general principles, you are more likely to strike gold in C.J.S.

The failure of Am. Jur. to cite cases from all jurisdictions is offset somewhat by the fact that the publisher of Am. Jur. also publishes legal encyclopedias for many individual states. For example, Bancroft-Whitney publishes a legal encyclopedia for California, California Jurisprudence, now in its third series (Cal. Jur. 3d). If you are searching for case cites in California, you could use Cal. Jur. 3d.

In order to do Ms. Smith's assignment, you could use either C.J.S. or Am. Jur., since she does not want a citation to every case but merely wants an overview.

There are two primary methods of finding relevant sections within C.J.S. and Am. Jur. Both encyclopedias contain a detailed word index in the last volumes of the set. Both also contain a table of contents for each topic.

Properly using the table of contents and index can require patience, sophistication, and a working knowledge of the legal vocabulary. You have been given a problem involving a landowner's negligence which resulted in injury on the landowner's property. In your torts course, you will learn that this type of a case involves what is called "premises liability." If you were to consult the index for Am. Jur. under "negligence — premises liability," it would direct you to see "Premises Liability (this index)."

Ms. Smith's problem also involves the question of whether the status of the injured person as a trespasser has anything to do with liability. The index for "Premises Liability" in Am. Jur. includes an entry for "Status of person injured," which directs you to read §§ 58-96 of the article titled "Premises Liability" in one of Am. Jur.'s main volumes. Similar efforts in C.J.S. would produce similar results.

It can be frustrating to use Am. Jur. and C.J.S. when you are unfamiliar with the general subject matter and the legal terminology used. And even when you know the general subject matter, the editors of Am. Jur. and C.J.S. may have used different words to describe what you are looking for. A good index will accommodate many different terminologies, but there is always the possibility of a mismatch. That is why you need to exercise some creativity, as well as patience, when using any index. If what you are looking for does not appear at first, try to reformulate your issue in different terms and keep looking.

2. Other Encyclopedias

In addition to these nationally known encyclopedias, many authors have published encyclopedias concerning the law of a particular jurisdiction. These encyclopedias may be much more influential within your jurisdiction than the nationally known encyclopedias, largely because of the local stature of the author. For example, Bernard Witkin of the San Francisco Bar has published a series of encyclopedias about California law that are often cited by California courts. His flagship encyclopedia, Summary of California Law, is now in its ninth edition. You should take a moment in your library to discover whether there exists a similar encyclopedia for your state.

E. American Law Reports, Annotated (A.L.R.)

Another useful source for finding the law around the country on a particular point of law is American Law Reports, Annotated ("A.L.R."), published by Lawyers Cooperative Publishing. Unlike C.J.S. and Am. Jur., A.L.R. is not organized systematically by topic. Instead, the articles in A.L.R. are organized by date of publication. A.L.R. is now in its forth series, and many of its earlier articles have been superseded by later articles.

At the beginning of every article is an opinion by a court in a particular case. That opinion is followed by an article concerning the legal issue discussed in the opinion. The article is comprehensive, citing all cases pro and con from all jurisdictions. A.L.R. articles are thus a good source for finding relevant cases from around the country. The only trick is to find an article on a relevant topic. A.L.R. articles are very narrowly focused, so you need to find an article that is exactly on point in order to use A.L.R.

A.L.R. is heavily indexed. Until recently, each A.L.R. series (1st through 4th, plus an A.L.R. F. for federal cases) had its own alphabetical Quick Index. A.L.R. has recently published a comprehensive Index to Annotations that can now be used to find annotations in A.L.R.2d, A.L.R.3d, A.L.R.4th, and A.L.R. Fed. This index is supplemented by a pocket part that appears in the front of each index volume. In addition to this index, A.L.R. publishes its own digest of its annotations that is organized by legal subject matter and issue.

Once you have found a relevant article in A.L.R. you need to update it to find more recent cases, if any. This is unfortunately not a particularly easy task within the A.L.R. system, since there are several places you may need to look. For the more recent set of A.L.R. volumes, A.L.R.3d, A.L.R.4th and A.L.R. Fed., pocket parts are used to supplement the annotations in the volumes. For A.L.R.2d annotations, there is no pocket part, and you must consult a separate volume, the A.L.R.2d Later Case Service (which is itself updated by a pocket part). For A.L.R. (first series) annotations, you must consult the A.L.R. Blue Book of Supplemental Decisions.

In addition to finding more recent cases, you also need to determine whether an annotation has itself been superseded or supplemented by a more recent annotation. In order to do this, you should consult the Annotation History Table in the Index to annotations and its pocket part. This Table will tell you whether any annotation in the A.L.R. series (1st-4th and Fed) has been supplement or superseded by a later annotation.

Although the A.L.R. volumes are sometimes not as easy to use as the legal encyclopedias, they can be enormously helpful to your research if you can find a relevant annotation. The articles are well written, they clearly set forth majority and minority rules, and they contain the results of comprehensive research on narrow legal issues.

A.L.R. is available on LEXIS as one of its secondary sources. When you are having trouble finding an annotation in the printed version, you should give LEXIS a try.

F. The Restatements of Law

In the 1920s, in response to the jurisprudential challenge posed by the legal realists, who at the extreme believed that law was whatever the individual judges happened to say it was on a particular day, a group of more traditional legal scholars formed the American Law Institute ("ALI"), whose mission was to discover and restate the law existing at the time in a series of black-letter sections and comments. The Restatement movement was inspired by the notion that law is not, as the realists sometimes claimed, whatever decision a judge happens to come up with, but rather, that the decisions reached by judges in individual cases reflected a set of more or less consistent and reasonable rules. There are Restatements for the following legal subjects: Agency, Conflict of Laws, Contracts, Judgments, Property, and Torts, among others.

Reflecting the philosophical view that law is reducible to a set of more or less consistent rules, the Restatements contain black-letter rules of law in sections. The black-letter rules are supplemented by comments and illustrations. The black-letter sections and comments are drafted by a Reporter with the assistance of several advisers. Drafts are then presented at yearly ALI meetings where the drafts are discussed and voted upon by the members. A majority vote is sufficient to ratify the work of the Reporter.

Restatements have been very popular with the bar and bench. There are a number of reasons for the success. First, the Reporters chosen for the Restatements have generally been some of the most respected scholars in their particular field. Since the work of the Reporter is reviewed by the ALI members, all of whom are also respected lawyers, judges and scholars, the Restatements have an aura of credibility about them. More important, however, is the fact that the Restatements have generally been of a very high quality, and courts have therefore quite often relied upon the Restatements in reaching decisions. The result is that Restatements (and especially those sections of a Restatement that have been explicitly adopted by a court) are a special kind of secondary authority — somewhere above a treatise but just below primary authority (i.e., the cases themselves). It is fair to say that you have not done complete research unless you have consulted an applicable Restatement, if one exists.

There are two ways to find relevant sections in a Restatement: First, there is an index in the back of each Restatement; second, and perhaps even more useful, there is a Table of Contents. The Restatements are generally organized in a logical legal sequence. For example, the Restatement (Second) of Contracts deals in Chapter 1 with the "Meaning of Terms" (such as "contract," "promise," and "agreement"); Chapter 2 is titled "Formation of Contracts — Parties and Capacity;" Chapter 3 is titled "Formation of Contracts — Mutual assent" (which includes sections on offer and acceptance). Subsequent chapters deal with consideration, the Statute of Frauds, and mistake, among other things. Thus, if you know generally what type of legal issue you are dealing with, you can usually use the Table of Contents to find an applicable section.

Let's return to the *Basso* problem by way of illustration. The general subject matter of *Basso* is the duty of care owed by landowners to people on their property. The Restatement (Second) of Torts is divided into Divisions: Division One concerns intentional torts; Division Two concerns negligence; Division Three concerns Strict Liability; and so on. *Basso* is a negligence case, so you would begin your search under Division Two.

Each Division is then divided into Chapters. Chapter 12 (the first chapter in Division Two), concerns General Principles of Negligence. Chapter 13 concerns Liability for Condition and Use of Land. *Basso* is most directly related to Chapter 13, and, indeed, you would find in Chapter 13 a review of the law of landowner liability.

Your research for Ms. Smith would definitely not be finished by looking at the Restatement since the Restatement (Second) of Torts was published in 1965. Thus, the Restatement is at least 20 years out of date. The black-letter in a Restatement may not be a reliable indication of what the law is today. There are two ways to update the law found in Restatement sections. First, there is a set of Shepard's volumes for the Restatements. You can use Shepard's to find all citations to a particular section. Second, ALI itself publishes an Appendix for each Restatement that includes annotations to cases citing and discussing Restatement sections.

.Even updating a Restatement section would not be the end of your research, however, since there may well be decisions that are important to your research that do not cite any Restatement section and would not appear in either the Restatement Shepard's or the Restatement Appendix. Thus, in order to compete your research, you will have to update any cases and law you may find with other sources, such as Shepard's or the digests.

The Restatement's are available on LEXIS and WESTLAW.

G. Treatises

Treatises are practitioner-oriented books that explain in detail the law relating to a particular subject matter. Reading a good treatise is an excellent way to educate yourself about general legal rules and concepts that may be applicable to your problem. Once you have a general understanding from the treatise, your comprehension of the cases, and the remainder of your legal research on a problem, will be greatly enhanced.

Treatises vary enormously in the depth of their coverage and in their quality. Some treatises purport to cover all cases relating to the subject matter; other treatises discuss only leading or important cases. Some treatises are supplemented with pocket parts or soft-bound supplements; other treatises are not supplemented at all, but are updated with a completely new edition. As you might expect, some treatises are also much more influential than others.

Because of these differences between treatises, your selection of a treatise is of critical importance. If you have never researched a particular field of law before, you should first survey the available treatises to determine which treatise is likely to be most helpful to you. As you probably know by now, for example, Allan Farnsworth's contracts treatise is well regarded by the courts, largely because of Farnsworth's stature (including the fact that he was a reporter for the Restatement (Second) of Contracts). Your reference librarian can help you select the best treatises available.

Some treatises, particularly multi-volume treatises, purport to be comprehensive in their depth of coverage. These treatises (for example, Moore's multi-volume treatise on Federal Practice) are not only a useful source for understanding the rules of civil procedure, but are also an excellent source for finding all of the relevant cases.

For Ms. Smith's research problem, you would want to consult a torts treatise. Several good treatises are available, but the two leading treatises are Harper and James' multi-volume set and Prosser and Keeton on Torts, now in its fifth edition. Either source would have a general review of the law respecting duties owed to trespassers.

H. Law Reviews

Law reviews generally contain articles written by scholars and students. The articles in any one issue may range from an overview of general principles in a particular field of law to an article discussing the decision reached in a single case (typically called case notes).

Coverage by law review articles is extremely variable. Some authors are of course better than others. Moreover, there is a wide degree of variation between articles by professional authors and articles by students. This is not to say that all students articles are less valuable than all professional articles. To the contrary, you may often find that a particular student article is much more useful to you than a professional article on the same topic. The difficulty, however, is knowing which articles are good and which are not so good. And you have no way of knowing about the quality of an article unless you read the entire article.

As a consequence of these factors, research into law reviews is generally a hit or miss venture. Sometimes you will be lucky, particularly if you are interested in a "cutting edge" development in the law; more often, you will come up empty handed. In most situations, you should begin your research somewhere else (for example, with treatises) and use law reviews to round out your research.

There are two main strategies for finding law review articles. First, courts will sometimes refer to law review articles in their decisions. You should read those articles, especially if the court quotes from or heavily relies upon an article. The second strategy is more systematic. The Index to Legal Periodicals and the Current Law Index are two sets of indexes to law review publications. Each set has a subject matter, author, statute, and case index. The statute and case index are particularly helpful if you want to determine whether an article has been written about a specific case.

An increasing number of law reviews are now available on LEXIS and WESTLAW. Searching through these databases can be a useful way of finding relevant materials.

I. Casebooks

During your remaining years in law school, you will spend many hours of your time reading casebooks. Indeed, you may find yourself reading little else besides casebooks. You should not, however, get the impression that casebooks will be of value to you in doing research or in practicing law after you have graduated. Casebooks are, in fact, practically useless for doing serious research. The reason is simple. Casebooks are written to teach more or less general principles. They are usually not written to be comprehensive either in scope of coverage or in depth of presentation. Indeed, even the text of the main cases in casebooks may not be reliable since they often have been heavily edited by the authors. You should not use casebooks in doing legal research either while in law school or once you have graduated.

J. Citation Notes for Secondary Authority

In order to find the proper citation forms for secondary sources, you need to consult the index in the back of the Blue Book. There are slightly different citation forms for each source.

Both C.J.S. and Am. Jur. are cited by volume number, topic name, section number, and, if necessary for clarity, page number. For example: 88 C.J.S. Trial § 192 (1955); 62 Am. Jur. 2d Premises Liability § 58, p. 302 (1971). Blue Book Rule 15.5.4. The citation form for an A.L.R. annotation is slightly different: Annotation, Modern Status of Rules Conditioning Landowner's Liability Upon Status of Injured Party as Invitee, Licensee, or Trespasser, 22 A.L.R.4th 294 (1981). Blue Book Rule 16.1.4.

Restatements of law are cited simply by the name of the restatement and its section: citing to a comment, that information should be added to the citation: Restatement (Second) of Torts § 402A, comment a (1965). Blue Book Rule 12.8.5.

Treatises are cited simply by the name of the author, the title, and the page number: Prosser & Keeton, Prosser on Torts § 15, p. 103 (1984 5th ed.). For multi-volume works, the number of the volume is generally put at the front of the citation: 21 C. Wright & K. Graham, Federal Practice and Procedure § 5023 (1977). Blue Book Rule 15.

Law reviews are cited by author, title, volume number, law review identifier, and page number: Cox, *Federalism and Individual Rights*, 73 Nw. U.L. Rev. 1 (1978). Blue Book Rule 16.

CHAPTER 6

SOURCES OF LEGISLATIVE LAW

In Chapters 2–5, we examined the sources of the common law. In the next two chapters, we will be examining "positive law." The phrase "positive law" refers to written rules enacted by some authoritative body (such as a legislature) which a court is bound to follow.

Positive law includes laws and rules promulgated at both the federal and the state level. Within each of these levels, there are many institutions which are empowered to make positive law. Let's start at the federal level.

A. Federal Legislation

The Supremacy Clause of the United States Constitution provides that

> "this Constitution, and the Laws of the United States which shall be made in Pursuance thereof; and all Treaties made, or which shall be made, under the Authority of the United States, shall be the supreme Law of the Land." Constitution, Art. VI.

By this provision, the Constitution identifies the three types of positive federal law: (1) The Constitution itself; (2) Treaties; and (3) Laws made in pursuance of the Constitution. Because the Supremacy Clause makes each of these "the supreme Law of the Land," both federal and state courts are duty-bound to give effect to controlling federal positive law.

In this and the next chapter, we shall focus our attention upon statutes and administrative regulations, which are laws made "in Pursuance" of the Constitution. Chapter 8 concentrates upon researching issues of constitutional law. Chapter 9 contains an introduction to the sources of international law, including treaties.

The Constitution provides the exclusive method by which laws are made:

> "Every Bill which shall have passed the House of Representatives and the Senate, shall, before it become a Law, be presented to the President of the United States; If he approve he shall sign it, but if not he shall return it, with his Objections to that House in which it shall have originated, who shall enter the Objections at large on their Journal, and proceed to reconsider it. If after such Reconsideration two thirds of that House shall agree to pass the Bill, it shall be sent, together with the Objections, to the other House, by which it shall likewise be reconsidered, and if approved by two thirds of that House, it shall become a Law. But in all such Cases the votes of both Houses shall be determined by Yeas and Nays, and the Names of the Persons voting for and against the Bill shall be entered on the Journal of each House respectively. If any Bill shall not be returned by the President within ten Days (Sunday

excepted) after it shall have been presented to him, the Same shall be a Law, in like Manner as if he has signed it, unless the Congress by their Adjournment prevent its Return, in which Case it shall not be a Law." Constitution, Art. I, § 7.

This procedure is the ultimate fountainhead of authority for all federal statutes and administrative regulations. We begin with the books and publications that contain the Laws and other enactments of Congress. As you might imagine, these major sources of law are available on both LEXIS and WESTLAW.

1. Finding the Text of Statutes and Other Acts of Congress

a. Slip Laws

Six months into the First Session of the first Congress, Congress enacted legislation to provide for the public dissemination of acts of Congress. Chapter 14, passed on September 15, 1789, provided that, whenever a bill became law,

"the [Secretary of State] shall, as soon as conveniently may be ... cause every such law, order, resolution, and vote, to be published in at least three of the public newspapers printed within the United States, and shall also cause one printed copy to be delivered to each Senator and Representative of the United States, and two printed copies duly authenticated to be sent to the Executive authority of each State." 1 Stat. 68.

Under the authority of this provision, the Secretary of State published each law in pamphlet form and then distributed each law in accordance with the statute. The printed copies published by the Secretary of State were known as "slip laws."

Slip laws are still published today. As soon as a law is enacted, the Government Printing Office will print the text and distribute it nationwide. Generally speaking, this official version of the slip law will arrive at law libraries after an unofficial version has been published (we will discuss these unofficial publications later).

b. Statutes at Large

The same statute that provided for the publication of slip laws also provided that laws were "to be recorded in books to be provided for the purpose." 1 Stat. 68. This was the first in a series of laws regulating the publication of the laws of the United States in book form.

During the Third Congress, in 1795, Congress enacted more detailed legislation to provide "for the more general promulgation of the laws of the United States." The act provided that:

"The Secretary for the department of State shall, after the end of the next session of Congress, cause to be printed and collated at the public expense, a complete edition of the laws of the United States, comprising the constitution of the United States, the public acts then in force, and the treaties, together with an index to the same." 1 Stat. 443.

Four thousand five hundred copies of that first edition were printed. In subsequent years, Congress made similar provisions for the publication of the laws in force.

The volumes published by the Secretary of State has neither indexes nor any cross-references between related legislation. This made it difficult to do systematic statutory research. A lawyer basically had to read all of the volumes to know what laws remained in force.

In 1845, the confusion engendered by the unsystematic publication of the laws led to a new version of the laws of the United States. In that year, Congress enacted legislation which provided, in part, "that the Attorney General is hereby authorized and directed to contact, on behalf of the General Government, with Messieurs Little and Brown, for one thousand copies of their proposed edition of the Laws and Treaties of the United States." 5 Stat. 799.

This new version, published by Little and Brown, was titled "Statutes at Large." Statutes at Large is cited by volume and page number (e.g., 5 Stat. 788). The title page describes the scope and contents of the work:

> "The Public Statutes at Large of the United States of America, from the Organization of the Government in 1789, to March 3, 1845. Arranged in Chronological Order. With References to the Matter of Each Act and to the Subsequent Acts on the Same Subject, and Copious Notes of the Decisions of the Courts of the United States Construing Those Acts, and upon the Subjects of the Laws. With an Index to the Contents of Each Volume, and a Full General Index to the Whole Work, in the Concluding Volume."

The first 8 volumes of Statutes at Large contain, in chronological order, the work of Congress from 1787 to 1845. The original editor of Statutes at Large, Richard Peters, wanted to organize statutes at large by subject matter, but his plan was thwarted by the Attorney General of the United States who was of the opinion that the act of Congress providing for the publication of Statutes at Large left no room for such a reorganization. The result was that the acts of Congress were printed in chronological order. Mr. Peters tried to overcome this less than convenient form by heavily indexing the volumes in accord with his proposed organization. There is an index by subject matter and title within each volume, and volume 8 contains an index for the entire set of volumes.

Because of the chronological order, however, it was at times difficult to be sure that the statute being looked at was all of the relevant law on a particular subject, despite Mr. Peter's generally complete cross-references to related statutory materials and to decisions by courts construing each section. If the acts of Congress had been organized by subject matter and had been continuously updated, then a lawyer could be relatively certain that all of the positive law on a particular subject had been found.

Statutes at Large is still published today by the Government Printing Office pursuant to the following legislation:

> "The Administrator of General Services shall cause to be compiled, edited, indexed, and published, the United States Statutes at Large which shall contain all the laws and concurrent resolutions enacted during each regular session of Congress; all proclamations by the President in the numbered series issued since the date of the adjournment of the regular session of Congress next

preceding; and also any amendments to the Constitution of the United States proposed or ratified pursuant to article V thereof since that date. . . ." 1 U.S.C. § 112 (1982).

It was apparent to some early on that Statutes at Large was not a particularly useful series of volumes because of its lack or organization and because it contained much outdated material. It collected all of the laws in one place and indexed that material, which had never before been done, but it did not impose a systematic structure upon those laws.

The confusion created by the many volumes of Statutes at Large led to a movement to revise the laws of the United States and, in the process of revision, to produce a single large volume containing all laws then in force. Congress acted in 1874 to do just that. After a long process of preparation, Congress enacted the Revised Statutes, whose purpose it was "to revise and consolidate the statutes of the United States, in force on the first day of December anno Domini one thousand eight hundred and seventy-three." 1 Rev. Stat. 1.

To understand what the Revised Statutes contains, we need to distinguish between a "revision" and a "compilation." A compilation of laws includes every piece of legislation enacted by Congress. The Statutes at Large is a compilation.

A revision, by contrast, is a selection of only those laws still in force and that are of interest to the public generally. By 1874, quite a few laws had been repealed outright. Such laws would appear in a compilation (along with the law of repeal). But in a revision, repealed laws are discarded. Other laws enacted by Congress lapse by their own provisions. Such a law would be included in a compilation, but not in a revision.

Finally, there are some laws that are of absolutely no interest to the public at large. They are "private" laws. The fact that our Congress still enacts such private legislation is something of an historical relic from the days when parliament and the congress of the Articles of Confederation actually sat as a judicial body in individual cases. As explained in a leading work on legislation of the 19th century:

"A public bill is one which operates upon some subject or measure of public policy in which the whole community is interested. A private bill is one which is for the particular interest or benefit of some person or persons, whether an individual or a number of individuals, a public company or corporation, a parish, city, county, or other locality having not a legal but a popular name only. In strictness, a private bill is one which, as regards the interest of the parties, is exceptional to the general law, so far as the particular subject of it is concerned; or which makes, or allows the parties to make, other and different arrangements, in reference to some particular matter, than would be authorized or allowed by the general law." L.S. Cushing, Law and Practice of Legislative Assemblies 297 (9th ed. 1874)

Public and permanent laws were published in Revised Statutes. Private or temporary acts were not included. The first edition of Revised Statutes (cited as R.S.) was published in 1872. It is one volume of 1092 pages, and it contained all public laws then in force.

The first edition of Revised Statutes was so successful that a second edition was published in 1878 incorporating new laws enacted by Congress in the intervening 6 years. This edition, in contrast to the first edition, was not enacted by Congress into positive law. Accordingly, the text appearing in the second edition of Revised Statutes is only "prima facie" evidence of United States law. This means that if there are any differences between what appears in the second edition and in the first edition or in Statutes At Large, the official text controls.

Interest waned in publishing any more revisions. For the next 50 years or so, the laws of the United States could be found only by consulting the Revised Statutes (first and second editions), supplements to Revised Statutes that were published in 1891 and 1901, and Statutes at Large.

c. United States Code

It was not until the last few years of the 19th century that lawyers again demanded that something be done about the confused state of our federal positive law. These demands ultimately led (after a series of false starts and incomplete projects) to the publication of the United States Code of 1925. The United States Code is today the primary source which you will use in your legal research to find the text of federal laws.

A code is a systematically organized version of laws in force at any one time. Efforts to codify laws in the United States began in the states in the middle 1800's. The most famous codifier from that time was David Field whose codification of New York's penal law, known as the Field Code, was used as a model by many states for the creation of systematic legislation.

The preface to the 1925 edition of the United States Code explains its historic significance:

> "This Code is the official restatement in convenient form of the general and permanent laws of the United States in force December 7, 1925, now scattered in 25 volumes — i.e., the Revised Statutes of 1878, and volumes 20 to 43, inclusive, of the Statutes at Large. No new law is enacted and no law repealed. It is prima facie the law. It is presumed to be the law. The presumption is rebuttable by production of prior unrepealed Acts of Congress at variance with the Code." The Code of Laws of the United States of America, preface. *See also* 44 Stat. 1.

The United States Code of 1925 contained 50 different "titles" (such as, General Provisions, Agriculture, Banks and Banking, Copyrights, Internal Revenue Code, and so forth) in 1700 pages of text. The laws in force relevant to each title were assembled in sequentially numbered sections. To cite to a particular provision in the United States Code, you therefore must have both the title number and the section number (e.g., 2 U.S.C. § 285 refers to Title 2 of the United States Code, Section 285).

As Congress enacts new laws, those laws are incorporated into the existing code which is supplemented by paper-bound and hardbound volumes. Every 6 years or so, an entirely new set of hardbound volumes, incorporating all of the changes made since the prior version, is published. The most recent edition was published in 1988. and the most recent Supplement as of November 1994 was published in 1993. The official edition is regularly behind, and that is one reason to use one of the unofficial versions of the United States Code.

Certain titles of the United States Code have now actually been enacted into positive law by act of Congress. These particular titles are therefore no longer merely "prima facie" evidence of the laws of the United States; they are the law itself. The other titles that have not been enacted into law are only "prima facie" evidence of the law. As mentioned before, this means that if there is a difference between the Statutes at Large text and the United States Code text (and mistakes do happen), the Statutes at Large text controls. At the beginning of each volume of the United States Code appears a page listing all fifty titles and indicating which of those titles have been enacted as law.

The work of codification is currently done by the Office of the Law Revision Counsel, established by Congress in 1974. 2 U.S.C. § 285, *et seq*. The Counsel is charged with keeping the United States Code updated.

In addition to containing the most recent version of the law, the United States Code has an extremely detailed index, and each title has a table of contents. With these finding aids, it is usually not a difficult task to find any statutes relevant to a particular legal issue or fact pattern.

d. United States Code Annotated

The United States Code is, for the titles enacted into law, the official law of the United States. The titles not formally enacted into law are "prima facie evidence" of the laws of the United States. United States Code Annotated (U.S.C.A.) is an unofficial version of the United States Code. It is neither the law nor even prima facie evidence of the law. You should therefore never cite U.S.C.A. to a court.

The U.S.C.A. is published by West. U.S.C.A. contains all of the same statutes that appear in U.S.C. U.S.C.A. also contains in its first volumes the Constitution. The volumes of U.S.C.A. are the same color as the volumes of U.S.C., but don't let yourself be confused by that. U.S.C.A. is an unofficial version, and you should always cite a court to U.S.C., the official version.

The primary advantage of U.S.C.A. over U.S.C. is that it contains case annotations (called "Notes of Decisions") for each section of the Code as well as for the Constitution itself. As cases are decided, the annotations are supplemented with monthly pocket parts. U.S.C.A. also gives some legislative history references (more about that later in this chapter) and references to other research aids published by West (such as Corpus Juris Secundum and the Digest system). The more recently published volumes also contain cross-references to a small number of non-West publications, such as law reviews. Finally, U.S.C.A. contains the usual sort of indexes and tables to facilitate finding relevant statutes

There are two steps in updating your research in U.S.C.A. First, each volume of U.S.C.A. has either a pocket part or a soft-bound supplementary pamphlet. These supplements include both revisions to the text of the statute and more recent case annotations. They are issued yearly. Second, at the end of the last volume of U.S.C.A., you should find one or more U.S.C.A. pamphlets published every four months that supplement the entire set of U.S.C.A. volumes during the year. Thus, to be completely current, you must check both a pocket part and the U.S.C.A. pamphlet service.

e. United States Code Service

United States Code Service (U.S.C.S.), published by Lawyers Cooperative Publishing, is another unofficial version of the United States Code and Constitution. Like U.S.C.A., U.S.C.S. contains a detailed index and table of contents. It also contains case annotations and citations to legislative history.

There are differences between U.S.C.A. and U.S.C.S., of course. U.S.C.S. does not cross-reference to West key numbers or to Corpur Juris Secundum. Instead, U.S.C.S. contains cross-references to other Lawyers Cooperative publications, such as American Jurisprudence and American Law Reports, Annotated. U.S.C.S. contains cross-references to relevant administrative rules and decisions. U.S.C.S. also contains rich cross-references to relevant law review articles and other secondary sources.

Like U.S.C.A., U.S.C.S. is supplemented by several publications. First, each volume contains a pocket part or soft-bound supplement. Second, U.S.C.S. publishes a cumulative supplement entitled the Cumulative Later Case and Statutory Service. Finally, U.S.C.S. has an advance service which indicates very recent changes to the statutory text (but does not include case annotations). This service includes a Table of Code Sections Added, Amended, Repealed, or Otherwise Affected, which you can use to determine whether your statute has been affected by recent congressional acts. Unlike the Cumulative Service, the Advance Service is not cumulative, and you must therefore look through all of the advance service sheets.

Because of the differences in coverage between U.S.C.A. and U.S.C.S., you may need to look at both sources when doing a research problem. U.S.C.A. can get you to C.J.S. and can give you a key number; in addition, the U.S.C.A. annotations to court decisions appear to be more comprehensive. On the other hand, U.S.C.S. can give you citations to other secondary sources not cited in U.S.C.A. and will cite relevant administrative agency decisions.

2. Shepard's for Statutes

In addition to these sources for finding cases and updating statutes, you may consult the Shepard's volumes for Statutes (Either U.S.C. citations or Statutes at Large citations) and the Constitution. These volumes work in pretty much the same way as Shepard's for cases. The Shepard's are comprehensive, citing every case that had cited a particular statute. Shepard's also includes citations to law review articles, presidential proclamations, and a host of other sources (such as A.L.R. annotations). As with Shepard's for cases, you will probably need to consult several volumes, including both Gold and Red supplements.

3. Citation Form for Federal Statutes

The rules regarding citation for statutes are rather intricate. Blue Book Rule 12. In general, however, you should cite only to U.S.C, the official code. Cites to U.S.C. include the title number, the section number, and the publication year for the set of U.S.C. volumes you are citing, which should generally be the most recent set of volumes: 42 U.S.C. § 1981 (1982). Blue Book Rule 12.3. The citation form for U.S.C.A. and U.S.C.S. is similar.

There will be times, however, when you will need to cite to Statutes at Large or to some other source. For example, if the text in U.S.C. differs from the text in Statutes at Large and the title of U.S.C. has not been enacted into positive law, you should cite to the Statutes at Large version with a note about the differences in the language. A Statutes at Large cite generally includes the title of the statute, a chapter number, the volume of Statutes at Large, the page within Statutes at Large, and the year of enactment: e.g., White-Slave Traffic (Mann) Act, ch. 395, 36 Stat. 825 (1910) (codified as amended at 18 U.S.C. §§ 2421–2424 (1982)). Blue Book Rule 12.4.

B. Federal Legislative History

It is often said by courts and commentators that the process of interpreting the words of a statute is the process of determining legislative intent. *See, e.g., K Mart Corp. v. Cartier, Inc.*, 486 U.S. 281, 300 (1988) (Brennan, J., concurring in part and dissenting in part). The most important evidence of what the legislature intended is the statute itself. You thus must pay careful attention to every word in a statute as well as to any other related statutes. Before becoming a justice on the Supreme Court of the United States, Professor Felix Frankfurter gave his law students three rules regarding statutory interpretation: READ THE STATUTE, READ THE STATUTE, READ THE STATUTE.

Words of course can take on a wide variety of meanings, and a court must often decide between two equally plausible interpretations of a particular statute. Although a court certainly could limit itself to a consideration of only the words of the statute, most courts will consider facts extrinsic to the statute if the extrinsic facts are probative of legislative intent. A legislative history is a collection of such extrinsic facts.

There are many things that could be part of a complete legislative history, including such things as newspaper stories published contemporaneously with passage of the legislation. The most authoritative sources, however, are found in official congressional documents, such as Senate and House reports, prior versions of the legislation, amendments adopted or rejected, statements made of the floor of Congress in support of or against the legislation, and so forth. We will discuss only these official documents.

Probably the most authoritative source of legislative intent, apart from the statute itself, are the reports of the Senate and House committees that considered the legislation prior to its passage. There may also be sub-committee reports that should be consulted. Any comments made about the legislation on the House or Senate floor will have been reported in the Congressional Record, which contains, among other things, a transcript of proceedings on the floor of Congress.

For about one hundred and fifty years, these official materials were virtually inaccessible to the ordinary lawyer. House and Senate documents were not widely available, and even when available, were so poorly indexed that doing research into the legislative history was prohibitively expensive. Thus, as late as 1947, there were textbooks on legal research that did not even suggest methods of finding sources of legislative history. The change began in 1941 with a new West publication.

1. United States Code Congressional and Administrative News (U.S. Code Cong. & Admin. News).

In 1941, West began publishing its multi-volume set titled United States Code Congressional and Administrative News ("USCCAN"). In the early volumes, West published the text of public laws from Statutes at Large and, in a separate part, included "Congressional Comments," which were excerpts from the legislative history. For the first time in our history, pieces of the legislative history and, more importantly, citations to the legislative history, became widely reported. West's Congressional Comments were so popular with the bar that West soon began to publish unedited versions of selected Senate or House reports plus citations to all relevant Senate and House documents and to the Congressional Record.

Finding the right volume and page within USCCAN is a trivial task. The statutes in USCCAN are published in the same order as Statutes at Large. If you have a Stat. cite, you can easily find the page in USCCAN where the text of the statute begins. That page will then give you a cross-reference to the appropriate page in the legislative history section of USCCAN. Alternatively, if you have a U.S.C. cite, simply look up the statute in U.S.C.A. which, since it is a West publication, contains a direct cross-reference to the legislative history in USCCAN.

You will have to use your library skills to find legislative documents that are not printed in USCCAN. Some federal depository libraries have a complete set of congressional reports as well as many congressional hearings in book form. A greater number of libraries have these materials available on microfiche. If your library simply does not have certain material that you need, you will have to look at other libraries. When all else fails, you can call the Library of Congress or the Government Printing Office to order specific material.

2. Congressional Information Service (C.I.S.)

In 1970, Congressional Information Service, Inc., began publishing a multi-volume set called Congressional Information Service ("CIS") that assembles in one place citations to virtually all official documents that would make up a complete legislative history. CIS is more comprehensive than USCCAN since it includes committee hearing reports and sub-committee reports and hearings, if available. CIS also includes cross-references to legislative materials pertaining to related statutes. It is the research tool of choice for post-1970 statutes.

There are several ways of accessing materials in CIS. For starters, CIS is indexed by public law number. You can get the public law number for a particular statute from, among other places, Statutes at Large, U.S.C., U.S.C.A. or U.S.C.S. The public law number is usually printed immediately after the text of the statute. CIS also has detailed subject matter indexes. This permits you to locate congressional documents on particular subjects even when you do not have a particular statue in mind.

In addition to obtaining citations to legislative history, CIS may be used to read the documents themselves. CIS publishes the documents in a comprehensive microfiche library probably located in the media room of your library. For recent legislation, you can fairly quickly compile a comprehensive legislative history from CIS.

C. State Statutes

Not surprisingly, state statutes are published in many of the same forms as federal statutes (and are available on both LEXIS and WESTLAW). Some states publish slip laws as they are enacted; in other states, a commercial publisher may publish an advance sheet that serves the same purposes as a slip law. All states publish session laws in a form similar to Statutes at Large. Every state jurisdiction also has a code similar to U.S.C. published either by the state or by a commercial publisher. Finally, virtually every state has an annotated code similar to U.S.C.A. or U.S.C.S. These annotated codes also include the state constitution and annotations to it.

The differences between the publication of federal and state laws are at the level of specific details. Some states, for example, use title and section numbers similar to the federal system. Other states use numbers and decimals (e.g., 1.331) to organize their laws. Some states (e.g., California) have divided the code into subject matter headings and refer to statutes by subject matter and section number (e.g., Cal.Evid.Code § 401). *See* Blue Book pp. 177–217 (containing sample citations for all state reporters and statutes).

Virtually all of your state statutory research is done using an annotated code, and you should familiarize yourself with the available annotated codes in your state. In California, for example, West publishes California Codes Annotated, and Bancroft-Whitney publishes Deering's California Code Annotated. You should examine both to determine which you prefer using, and, as with U.S.C.A. and U.S.C.S., you may find it helpful to consult both sets in your research.

As with the federal sources, you should identify the proper method of updating statutes. There typically will be both a pocket-part supplement for each volume and a cumulative supplement for all volumes. There also will be a Shepard's volume for each state's statutes.

It is only very recently that some state legislatures have begun to pay attention to preserving a legislative history for state statutes. In most states, it is nearly impossible to construct a legislative history for statutes enacted more than twenty or thirty years ago. The basic documents simply have not been preserved. Even finding the legislative history of a statute enacted a mere five or ten years ago can require supreme patience and diligence. Because it is so difficult to find state legislative history, businesses have opened in several states which do nothing but assemble legislative histories for paying clients (usually law firms).

Researching state legislative history will undoubtedly become easier in the information age. In California, for example, all legislative bills and reports are now publicly available on the Internet system. In time, it seems likely that all legislative materials will be available electronically, and assembling a complete legislative history will be as simple as requesting the right icon on the screen. Until that magic day arrives, however, we will have to make do with the sources presently available.

CHAPTER 7

SOURCES OF ADMINISTRATIVE LAW

In the previous chapters, you have been introduced to the sources of common law and statutory law. In this chapter, you will be introduced to the other main source of law in the United States, administrative law.

There is nothing in the Constitution that authorizes Congress to create administrative agencies and to give them the power to enact rules or decide cases. Until the beginning of this century, administrative agencies were virtually unheard of, at least in their present form. Although the Constitution does not expressly give Congress the power to create administrative agencies, it has generally been assumed that Congress has that power and that the large number of administrative agencies that exist have been constitutionally created pursuant to Congress' undoubted power to enact laws.

Administrative agencies make law in two ways. First, agencies are often given the power to enact rules that have the force of law. Second, agencies are often given the power to adjudicate claims that have been brought either by the agency against a private person or by one private person against another private person. An administrative agency thus exercises both quasi-legislative and quasi-judicial functions.

As with federal and state statutory materials, both LEXIS and WESTLAW have extensive administrative law databases.

A. Federal Regulations

1. Background of Rule-Making

Rule-making by an administrative agency is similar to law-making by Congress since both processes typically involve public hearings that ultimately may lead to the enactment of positive law. There are, however, more differences than similarities between rule-making and law-making. Prior to enactment of the Federal Register Act of 1935, 49 Stat. 500, rules enacted by administrative agencies were not systematically published in any form, and there was little opportunity for public input into the rule-making process. This was not a cause for much concern, however, since the number of agencies was relatively small.

During the Roosevelt presidency and the New Deal, however, the number of administrative agencies grew dramatically. As their power and influence expanded, it became necessary to formalize the procedures under which the agencies operated. Over a fifteen-year period (1935-1950), legislation was enacted that set forth procedural requirements for both rule-making and adjudication.

The statutory requirements imposed upon agency rule-making were designed to permit public comment on proposed rules before they came into effect and to insure that a rule was not enacted until there had been a full public hearing. The statutes thus require that a proposed rule be published, that the agency hold public hearings concerning the rule, that the agency report a tentative decision following those hearings, and that the agency consider any further public comment before formally promulgating the rule.

2. The Federal Register (Fed. Reg.)

The Federal Register Act of 1935, 49 Stat. 500, provides that executive orders and administrative regulations be published in a daily publication titled the "Federal Register." Prior to creation of the Federal Register, administrative regulations were not systematically collected anywhere. The Federal Register was designed to fill that gap, and its function was similar to Statutes at Large.

It soon became apparent that the Federal Register could be used more generally as a convenient medium of communication between administrative agencies and the public. With passage of the Administrative Procedure Act in 1946, the Federal Register was also used to report proposed rules in addition to enacted rules. 5 U.S.C. § 553. Today, the Federal Register may contain a variety of official announcements by the executive and by administrative agencies.

As with Statutes at Large, the Federal Register is not organized by subject matter. Material is published in the Federal Register in chronological order. Although each daily edition of the Federal Register has a Table of Contents, there is no general index to the Federal Register. As you might expect, then, the Federal Register is not a particularly useful research tool on its own; other sources must be used to locate material in the Federal Register.

The Federal Register is paginated sequentially throughout the year. Because the page numbers get rather high (e.g., 32543), it is more convenient to locate material in the Federal Register if you have the date of publication in addition to the page number. You can then more quickly find the page you are searching for. This process is made easier by a table of issue pages and dates that appears in a "Reader's Aid" section of each edition of the Federal Register.

3. The Code of Federal Regulations (C.F.R.)

Just as the United States Code was necessary to provide the public with an organized version of Statutes at Large, the Code of Federal Regulations was necessary to provide the public with an organized version of the Federal Register. The Code of Federal Regulations (C.F.R.) is generally organized into titles, parts, and sections. In a typical C.F.R. citation, 26 C.F.R. § 1.123, the number 26 is the Title number, and 1.123 is the section number. The section number is actually composed of two elements: the number 1 in "1.123" is the part number, and the number 123 in "1.123" is the section number within part 1. Section numbers within each part are numbered consecutively. Thus, 1.6 (Part 1, Section 6) appears before 1.121 (Part 1, Section 121) because 6 is less than 121 (even though the number "1.121" is smaller than the number "1.6").

Each title of C.F.R. is updated yearly with new volumes. Each year's volumes are a different color. For example, the 1993 C.F.R.'s are purple; and the 1994

C.F.R.'s are gray. Volumes of C.F.R. are shipped at various times throughout the year. Titles 1–16 are supposed to be shipped around January 1; Titles 17–27 are supposed to be shipped around April 1, and so forth. Thus, for most of the year, you will have two colors of C.F.R.'s on your shelves.

At the end of the set of C.F.R. volumes is an index. The index is not very detailed, and it refers you only to parts within a title. Once you have a part number, you must scan the table of contents for that part to find a relevant section. The index volume also includes a Table of parallel Authorities and Rules. This table gives you cross-references between rules and cross-references between U.S.C. sections and C.F.R. sections. This table helps you connect your statutory research with specific regulations.

A much more detailed and useful index to C.F.R. is published by R. R. Bowker and is called The Code of Federal Regulations Index. You will probably find that this unofficial index is much easier to use. Remember that you also can get references to C.F.R. sections from U.S.C.A. or U.S.C.S.

By using all the available aids, including the Federal Register, you can update a C.F.R. section to within one day before the day of your research. At the end of the C.F.R. volumes, you will find a number of volumes entitled "List of C.F.R. Sections Affected" ("L.S.A."). These volumes are published monthly and contain a list of all C.F.R. sections affected since the latest edition of the main C.F.R. volume. You need to look on the front of the most recent L.S.A. to determine whether it covers all changes from the publication of the main C.F.R. volume; there may be a gap in dates between the most recent L.S.A. and your C.F.R. volume. If there is, look at the other L.S.A. volumes to fill the gap. After looking at the relevant L.S.A. volumes, you can finish updating your research by consulting the most recent issues of the Federal Register.

If a particular C.F.R. section has been affected, L.S.A. will indicate the type of change (e.g., revised, added, or removed) and will identify the relevant page in the Federal Register. Each volume of L.S.A. contains a table of Federal Register pages and dates so you can convert the Federal Register page number to a date. You then can check the Federal Register to ascertain whether the change is relevant to your research. To finish the updating process, you need to consult the most recent edition of the Federal Register and check the table of C.F.R. sections affected.

Last, but not least, you need to check the Shepard's volume for C.F.R. to find any cases interpreting the regulation.

B. Federal Administrative Decisions

Federal administrative decisions are generally reported in an official reporter published by the government. For example, decisions by the Internal Revenue Service are published in United States Tax Court Reports; decisions by the National Labor Relations Board are published in N.L.R.B. Reports.

In order to find relevant administrative decisions from a particular agency, you will generally use a lose-leaf service that reports on the activities of that agency.

The two biggest publishers of loose-leaf services are CCH (Commerce Clearing House) and BNA (Bureau of National Affairs).

A loose-leaf service for a particular agency is typically a multi-volume set of ring binders. The service is kept up to date by replacing pages in the binders. A loose-leaf will generally report on both rule-making and adjudicatory activity. In order to find relevant administrative decisions, you simply need to find the section within the loose-leaf that digests the subject matter. That index usually will give you a page number within the loose-leaf service, and you will then find on that page a case digest.

Once you have found a relevant administrative decision, you need to update your research with the appropriate volume of Shepard's.

C. State Administrative Law

Administrative law at the state level is much less organized. Many states do not even require central publication of administrative regulations, and there are very few official or unofficial reports of state administrative adjudication. Some states are beginning to organize their administrative law, however. For example, California now publishes an Administrative Code that contains all regulations now in force. Nevertheless, research into state administrative law is definitely a hit or miss venture. Your knowledge of state administrative law is thus much more likely to be gained through the experience of working directly with a state administrative body than through research in the library.

CHAPTER **8**

CONSTITUTIONAL RESEARCH

Prior chapters have introduced you to research strategies appropriate for the different types of law and bibliographic sources that are available to you. Chapter 2 dealt with the common law, and Chapters 4 (digests) and 5 (secondary sources) dealt primarily with bibliographic sources that offer different ways of finding the common law. Chapters 6 and 7 dealt with legislative and administrative materials.

This chapter, dealing with constitutional research, is different because we are here interested in how to perform research in a field of law — constitutional law. This chapter could just as easily have been about tort research, contract research, or property law research, but the idea here is to present to you the challenge of attempting to perform research in a field of law about which you are likely to be relatively unaquainted. How do you perform legal research when you don't know much about the area of law being researched?

As you will see, the bibliographic sources used in performing constitutional research are essentially the same sources previously covered in chapters 2 through 7. Issues of constitutional law may arise in each context — in cases, in statutes, and in administrative regulations or decisions — and you will use digests, other secondary sources, and updating services, such as Shepard's, when doing constitutional research.

For purposes of this chapter, we shall limit our consideration to researching issues arising under the United States Constitution. Assume that your client, Jones, is an officer in the United States Navy who has been discharged as a result of publicly announcing that he is gay. The Navy's policy at the time of discharge was not to inquire about sexual orientation, but to discharge someone upon learning that the person was homosexual or had engaged in homosexual acts. Jones' voluntary disclosure of his sexual orientation to the Navy resulted in his discharge under this policy. Jones wants to know whether the Navy's policy is constitutional and whether he can be reinstated.

A. Bibliographic Sources for Constitutional Research

Whenever you are beginning to perform research in an unfamiliar field of law, the very first step is to identify the bibliographic sources which are available. Even without making a trip to the library, you can make some pretty confident predictions about the type of sources that should be available to you.

First, since the Constitution, like statutes, is positive law (i.e., it is a series of written rules), you should expect there to be a set of volumes containing the complete text of the Constitution with annotations to cases and other sources discussing each section. Your expectations would be met in both U.S.C.A. and U.S.C.S., both of which contain volumes devoted to the Constitution.

Second, you should expect Shepard's to have a special set of volumes devoted to citations to the Constitution. Again, you would not be disappointed.

Third, since the Supreme Court of the United States is the ultimate authority when it comes to interpreting the Constitution, you should expect the West and the Lawyers' Cooperative digests for the Supreme Court to be useful sources of information about constitutional law issues.

Fourth, given the importance of the Constitution and the significance of constitutional law as developed by the Supreme Court, there should be a wealth of secondary sources dedicated exclusively to the topic of constitutional law. C.J.S. and Am. Jur. should have constitutional law as a separate topic. There may be a separate encyclopedia devoted entirely to constitutional law. There should certainly be many treatises dealing with constitutional law. Maybe there is a Restatement of Constitutional Law.

In fact, a trip to library would confirm most of these predictions. C.J.S. and Am. Jur. contain constitutional law as a separate topic. There is an excellent encyclopedia for constitutional law titled, appropriately enough, Encyclopedia of the American Constitution, edited by L.W. Levy, K.L. Karst and D.J. Mahoney. This encyclopedia contains thousands of articles dealing with constitutional law issues.

As for treatises, looking up "constitutional law" in your library's card catalogue, you would find scores of references. Two of the most frequently cited are Professor Laurence Tribe's American Constitutional Law, now in its second edition, and a treatise by Professors John Nowak and Ronald Rotunda simply titled Constitutional Law, now in its fourth edition. These treatises contain citations to additional important secondary sources, including legislative histories of the Constitution, law review articles, annotations in A.L.R., and so forth.

Although the idea of a Restatement of Constitutional Law makes sense, in fact the American Law Institute has never produced such a restatement. The important thing, however, is that when you begin researching a new field of law, you should enter the library with an open mind about the bibliographic resources that might be available. You should, in other words, check to see whether there is a Restatement of Constitutional Law, or a Restatement of Environmental Law and Land Use, and so on. If you don't look for a source, you will never know whether it exists or not — unless you fortuitously encounter a reference to it in another source.

B. The Process of Constitutional Research

The problem in beginning your research is to know where to begin and how to proceed. When you are unfamiliar with an area of law, it is probably a mistake to begin your research by trying to find particular cases relevant to your problem by using, for example, a digest. The risk is that your lack of knowledge about the substantive law may impair your ability to search for cases (because, for example, you simply don't know the right legal terminology).

You should instead begin your research with a good treatise. Reading a few relevant sections or chapters in a treatise (or perhaps the entire treatise) should give you enough background knowledge to enable you to begin searching through cases.

(Matthew Bender & Co., Inc.)

The treatise may even give you citations to a few of the leading cases relevant to your problem, and, in any event, will give you the terminology that is likely to be used in both the digests and the cases. You will have learned enough from the treatise to know how to search for relevant decisions.

In order to begin research for your client, Jones, you might consult the index to Tribe's treatise under "gay" or "homosexual" or "sexual orientation." You would quickly find that Tribe has an entire section of his treatise, § 15–21, devoted to the topic of "The Future of Privacy and Personhood: Sex and Sexual Orientation." You could find a similar section, § 14.30, in Nowak and Rotunda's treatise dealing with "Right to Engage in Sexual Acts."

You would discover in both treatises a somewhat dense discussion about equal protection and rights of privacy and, in particular, a lengthy analysis of the Supreme Court's decision in *Bowers v. Hardwick*, 478 U.S. 186 (1986), where the Court upheld the constitutionality of Georgia's sodomy statute. *Bowers* thus seems to be contrary to the position you would like to take on behalf of your client. Both treatises cite many cases, but the cases cited — including *Bowers* — do not seem on their face to be factually close to the situation facing your client.

The fact that *Bowers* does not seem at first to be helpful should not cause you to become despondent. The fun is just beginning. Both treatises cite a 1985 Note published in the Harvard Law Review as providing a possible argument for striking down governmental discrimination against homosexuals. Note, *The Constitutional Status of Sexual Orientation: Homosexuality as a Suspect Classification*, 98 Harv. L. Rev. 1285 (1985).

Consulting this Note, you would discover that it does indeed advocate subjecting government rules that discriminate against homosexuals to a heightened form of judicial scrutiny called "strict scrutiny." Under strict scrutiny, most of these rules would be unconstitutional. Unfortunately, the Note again does not discuss in the text any cases that are factually similar — cases, for example, that involve the military.

But buried in footnote 101 of this article, the author notes that "Government discrimination against gay military personnel is widespread," citing *Dronenburg v. Zech*, 741 F.2d 1388 (D.C. Cir. 1984). Rushing to the Federal Reporter, Second Series, you would discover that *Dronenburg* is factually quite similar to your case, involving a Navy officer who was discharged as a consequence of his homosexuality. The court in *Dronenburg* upheld the discharge, but that of course is just one case. *Dronenburg* cites a decision from the Ninth Circuit Court of Appeals, *Beller v. Middendorf*, 632 F.2d 788 (9th Cir. 1980), *cert. denied*, 452 U.S. 905 (1981), that also involved a Navy discharge because of homosexuality. Unfortunately, the court in *Beller* also upheld the discharge.

Before telling your client that he is out of luck, however, you must update your research to determine if *Dronenburg* and *Beller* are still good law. If you had shepardized *Beller* on September 6, 1994, you would have discovered that the Ninth Circuit Court of Appeals distinguished *Beller* in a decision rendered on August 31, 1994, *Meinhold v. United States Department of Defense*, 1994 WESTLAW 467311 (9th Cir. 1994). In *Meinhold*, the court held that the Navy could not constitutionally discharge Meinhold, who did nothing more than announce publicly that he was gay, absent proof that Meinhold was likely to engage in prohibited homosexual acts. *Meinhold* gives you a basis for arguing that Jones' discharge was unconstitutional.

Your research at this point would be just beginning, but you would clearly be on the right track. You will have found a series of cases dealing with military discharges on account of sexual orientation, and those cases in turn give you plenty of citations to general principles of constitutional law that you would use to structure your argument.

The important lesson of this chapter and example is that legal research almost always involves using multiple sources, tracking down vague hints and suggestions, reading your sources thoroughly, and methodically updating whatever cases or statutes you find. Legal research is an activity, and it is an activity that requires focus, determination and patience. Someone who is easily discouraged might have stopped with *Bowers* or given up hope with *Dronenburg* and *Beller*. The competent researcher, however, is never satisfied until all of the stones have been turned over, and all of the i's dotted and t's crossed.

You should try to do this research assignment on LEXIS and WESTLAW. See what sort of a search request would find the right set of cases.

CHAPTER 9

TREATIES AND OTHER SOURCES OF INTERNATIONAL LAW

As recently as one hundred years ago, international law was primarily the domain of diplomats and those relatively few persons and businesses which operated across national boundaries. It was a rare event for a private practitioner to have need for researching issues of international law.

As a result of the dramatic improvements in transportation and communication technologies over the past half-century, we have seen an equally dramatic increase in the number and complexity of business and personal relationships that cross national boundaries. Transnational transactions are rapidly becoming the normal way of doing business for thousands of companies. These new, pervasive transnational relationships have created a pressing need for the development of new and relatively uniform rules of international law. We have seen in the past fifty years an explosion of international law.

There is, of course, no "world government" which has jurisdiction over all relationships between sovereign states. Although some have feared that the United Nations might be a step along the path towards a single world government, those fears appear to have been vastly overstated. The United Nations has become an important player in world affairs, particularly in the past ten or fifteen years, but its activities are far from constituting world government.

Because there is no formal world government and no single fount of international law, the sources of international law are diverse and not particularly systematic. According to Article 38(1) of the Statute of the International Court of Justice, international law encompasses, among other things,

"a. international conventions, whether general or particular, establishing rules expressly recognized by the contesting states;

b. international custom, as evidence of a general practice accepted as law;

c. the general principles of law recognized by civilized nations;

d. . . . judicial decisions and the teachings of the most highly qualified publicists of the various nations, as subsidiary means for the determination of rules of law." Statute of the International Court of Justice, Art. 38(1), 59 Stat. 1055.

The international conventions referred to in Article 38 include treaties and executive agreements entered into by the United States with other countries. International custom, general principles of law recognized by civilized nations, and the teachings of scholars constitute the other corpus of international law. We will deal first with United States treaties and executive agreements.

(Matthew Bender & Co., Inc.) (Pub. 776)

LEXIS has a particularly broad collection of international law materials available in library "intlaw".

A. United States Treaties and Executive Agreements

1. Introduction

Article II, § 2, of the Constitution provides that the President "shall have power, by and with the advice and consent of the Senate, to make treaties, provided two-thirds of the Senators present concur." A "treaty" is simply a binding agreement between two or more states in written form and governed in its interpretation and operation by international law. *See, e.g.,* Vienna Convention on the Law of Treaties, U.N. Doc. A/Conf. 39/27, Part I, Art. 2, ¶ 1(a) (1969), reprinted in 63 Am. J. Int'l L. 875 (1969).

In terms of the Constitution, treaties are, like statutes, "the supreme law of the land." Const., Art. VI, § 2. A treaty which is inconsistent with a previously enacted statute controls, and a treaty preempts any inconsistent state laws as well.

But since a statute is also the "supreme law of the land," a subsequently enacted statute which is inconsistent with a previously enacted treaty in effect repeals the treaty, at least insofar as American courts are concerned. A subsequent, inconsistent statute may breach the United States's obligation under the treaty pursuant to principles of international law, but "the supreme law of the land" will nevertheless be the statute instead of the treaty.

The President's foreign relations power is not limited to making treaties. Article II, § 2, also makes the President the "commander in chief" and gives the President the power to nominate, with the advice and consent of the Senate, ambassadors to represent the United States overseas. These provisions, along with the practical reality that foreign policy must be implemented by a relatively few number of persons at any one time, have resulted in making the President the undoubted leader in matters of foreign policy, even though this power is not expressly granted to the President.

The other practical reality is that a successful foreign policy often requires that the United States agree to enter into agreements with other sovereigns, and that the treaty process is a relatively cumbersome mechanism for entering into such agreements. The result has been a general acceptance of the President's power to enter into Executive Agreements with other sovereigns which have the effect of law notwithstanding the failure to seek or secure the Senate's concurrence. As just one example, the General Agreement on Tariffs and Trade ("GATT") is an Executive Agreement and not a treaty. Every now and then, some members of Congress assert that the President does not actually have the power under the Constitution to create binding obligations on behalf of the United States short of a treaty, but these objections are generally sporadic and have not commanded any significant, long-term support. As you might expect, Presidents have much more frequently employed their power to enter into Executive Agreements instead of treaties in order to avoid the politics of the treaty approval process.

2. Finding Treaties and Executive Agreements

The text of treaties and executive agreements can be found in a number of different sources, and the complete details are beyond the scope of this introductory text. Students who need to learn the details are encouraged to consult Chapter 15 of Morris L. Cohen, Robert C. Berring, and Kent C. Olson, How to Find the Law (9th ed. 1989).

For introductory purposes, however, the main sources can easily be identified. All treaties that have been ratified and executive agreements that have been entered into after 1950 may be found in the many volumes of United States Treaties and Other International Agreements (U.S.T). Before being published in the hardbound volumes of U.S.T., treaties are published first in pamphlet form in the Treaties and Other International Acts Series (T.I.A.S.). A complete collection of pre-1950 treaties may be found in Treaties and Other International Agreements of the United States, 1776-1949, which is published by the Department of State.

There are several indexes to these voluminous sets of treaties and other agreements. The Department of State annually publishes Treaties in Force which contains a listing of all treaties and agreements that are presently in force, with cross-references by country and subject matter. Another annual publication, A Guide to the United States Treaties in Force, contains a more detailed subject matter index. For pre-1950 treaties and agreements, you can consult the detail indexes in United States Treaties and Other International Agreements Cumulative Indexes, 1776-1949. Finally, the State Department publishes a monthly Department of State Bulletin which contains a section concerning any new treaty information during the prior month.

Treaties and agreements, like statutes, often need to be interpreted by courts, and you need to be able to find cases interpreting the provisions of a relevant treaty. Shepard's United States Citations has a section for United States Treaties and Other International Agreements. The United States Code Service also has a volume for uncodified laws and treaties which contains case annotations for treaties.

B. Other Sources of International Law

As noted above, the sources of international law include, in addition to formal agreements between sovereigns, international customary practice and general principles of international law. In establishing customary practice and general principles, we may rely to some extent upon judicial decisions rendered by the International Court of Justice and the views of respected scholars of international law.

The International Court of Justice (I.C.J.), which sits in the Hague and is an organ of the United Nations, hears only a few cases every year and is limited to hearing disputes between states. Although its decisions may be some evidence of customary practice or general principles of international law, decisions by the International Court of Justice are not binding beyond the parties before the court and do not become precedents. See Statute of the International Court of Justice, Art. 59, 59 Stat. 1055. The court's decisions are published in the I.C.J. Reports of Judgments, Advisory Opinions and Orders. Its decisions, as well as decisions rendered by other international tribunals such as the Court of Justice of the European Community, are also published in International Law Report (I.L.R.). As usual, there are a number of digests of I.C.J. opinions. For example, Case Law of the International Court, published by Sijthoff, contains excerpts from I.C.J. decisions from 1952 until the present.

There are a wealth of secondary sources dealing with issues of international law. The Department of State has sponsored publication of a series of digests of international law as viewed from the American perspective. The most recent set, beginning in 1973, is the Digest of United States Practice in International Law. It includes analyses of international law issues along with excerpts from treaties, judicial decisions and other relevant documents.

The American Law Institute has also weighed in with its views on certain aspects of international law in the Restatement of the Foreign Relations Law of the United States, now in its third edition.

There are a number of treatises dealing with particular aspects of international law. Two of the leading treatises are L. Oppenheim, International Law, and I. Brownlie, Principles of Public International Law (3d ed. 1979). There are also several introductory works geared specifically for the student market, including T. Buergenthal and H.G. Maier's Public International Law in a Nutshell (1985), and M.W. Janis's An Introduction to International Law (1988).

In addition to these treatises, there are quite a few good law reviews that are devoted entirely to international law issues. The two leading journals in the field are the American Journal of International Law and International Lawyer.

It is safe to say that researching issues of international law can be a frustrating experience. Oftentimes, you will discover that there is both too little material dealing with a specific questions you have and too much material dealing with generalities and principles. Worse yet, because international law issues arising outside the context of a treaty necessarily involve proof of international customs and generally accepted principles, it is extremely difficult to establish exactly what international law provides. You can quickly find yourself discussing questions like, "How many countries have to agree for there to be a custom?" "At what point does a principle become generally accepted?" There are no easy answers to these questions, which gives international law a more fluid feel than domestic law. Some find the extra flexibility exhilarating; others find it exhausting.

As a private practitioner, you will more likely find yourself involved in interpreting language contained in treaties or executive agreements. These issues call upon the same basic skills of analysis and research that you will be developing in the context of interpreting statutes and constitutional provisions.

One thing remains relatively certain. In today's shrinking world, you will be confronted relatively quickly in your legal career with issues arising under one or another of our international obligations.